OTPRINT

DELFT SCHOOL OF DESIGN JOURNAL

D0227776

S-DISCIPLINARY

N 2007

Grey Room
40

ARCHITECTURE AFTE

JUNKSPACE ○ ○

CONSENSUS ○ ○

IRONY ○ ○

PRACTICE ○ ●

OPPOSITIONS ○ ○

LANGUAGE ○ ○

BILBAO ○ ○

PEDAGOGY ○ ○

9/11 ● ○

MODERNISM ○ ○

URBANISM ○ ○

1968 ○ ○

HOLLAND ○ ○

FEMINISM ○ ○

CLASSICISM ● ○

FORM ○ ○

BLOB ○ ○

GLOBALIZATION ○ ●

POST-MODERNISM ○ ○

IMAGE ○ ○

FASHION ○ ○

AUTONOMY ● ○

NARRATIVE ○ ○

SIGNATURE ○ ○

TECHNOLOGY ○ ○

MARXISM ○ ●

ARVARD
SIGN
AGAZINE

Harvard Unive
Graduate Scho
Architecture
Landscape arch
Urban planning
Spring/Summe

32

THE FUNCTION OF ORNAMENT

EDITED BY FARSHID MOUSSAVI

MICHAEL KUBO

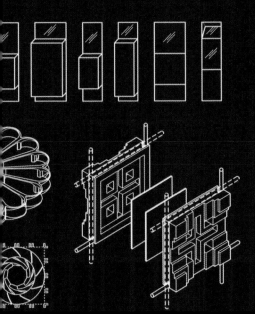
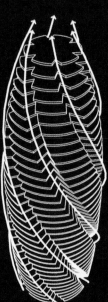

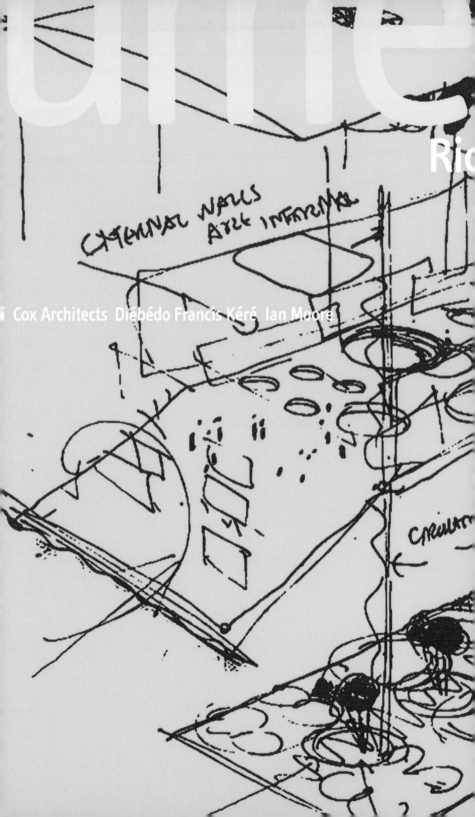

EXTERNAL WALLS ARE INFORMAL

Cox Architects Diébédo Francis Kéré Ian Moore

CIRCULAT

ARCHITEKTUR

Produktion und Gebrauch gebauter Umw

volur

Agitation

HUNC

The Berlage Institute Report on Architecture, Urbanism, and

THE SIGNIFIC

OF ARCHITEC

S CONSTRU

PUBLICIT

N THE COLL

IMAGINATI

Sust
and
Deve

306090 Books, Volume
Joshua Bolchover and J

BOLCHOVER, Joshua and
SOLOMON, Jonathan D.
EASTERLING, Keller
CUFF, Dana and
DAHL, Per-Johan
MAHER, Dennis
DORAN, Kelly
SCROGGIN, Jason
DRING, Alison and
SCHWAAG, Daniel

SVERDLOV, Alexander
SAMPLE, Hilary
BRAZIER, J. Cressica and
LAM, Tat
BOLCHOVER, Joshua and
LIN, John
DAVIS, Juliet
KOHN, David
DE LOOZ, Pierre Alexandre
JIANG Jun

AYON, Angel,
MARKS, Gerald, and
WHITE, Sarah
EDICK, Kipp,
HILLYARD, Chris, and
YUNG, Edward
MARSHALL, Victoria
BRACKEN, Gregory
HEMPEL, Adina
LI Shiqiao

bracl

architecture, enviro

[on farming [

Log

FALL 2008
Aftershocks:
Generation(s)
since 1968

13
—
14

Home is
the most
important
place in
the world.

MANIFOLD 3

inter, 2009 | The Interview Issue

MAR

—————————— ANOTHER ARCHITECTURE

20/20: EDITORIAL TAKES
ON ARCHITECTURAL DISCOURSE

20/20: EDITORIAL TAKES
ON ARCHITECTURAL DISCOURSE
Edited by Kirk Wooller

20/20

CONTENTS

NOTES FOR THE ARCHITECTURAL EDITOR IN AN AGE OF WORDPRESS
Preface by Brett Steele

Modern architectural culture has not been shaped by architects, at least, not in the sense we normally use the term architect, denoting an individual who commits the majority of his or her waking hours to the conceiving and drawing of architectural space, built form or the distribution of a client's programme of needs. To a remarkable degree, architectural culture has been shaped by one unique and distinctive kind of architectural mind: that of the architectural editor. Always strong and distinct, sometimes hidden and abiding, and increasingly threatened and undermined, architectural editors are the real makers of modern architectural culture. They are its architects; its shapers, its form-givers. And to a very large degree, its conscience.

What we think of as architectural culture today is the result of forces that converged in the early twentieth century around revolutionary architectural ideas and newly industrialised, print-based forms of modern media. For architecture this amounted to a rupture as much as an extension of its long-held bookish ways, and one that soon made the mass printing of words, drawings and photographs the dominant architectural technology of the twentieth century. Unsurprisingly, given the core skill-set demanded of an increasingly mediated (and industrialised) architectural world, the modern architectural editor was born. The figure soon emerged from within this communication infrastructure to become a unique kind of form-giver, one able to work as – and not only for – the architect.

As evidence of this, consider the formative experiences of architects working as editors during the past century,

from Frank Lloyd Wright's 1910 *Wasmuth Folio* (a 15-year
compilation of mid-career reinvention micro-managed by
the architect from his Oak Park studio) to Rem Koolhaas's
similarly mid-career effort released in 1995, titled *S,M,L,XL*.
Between these two bookish ends of the twentieth century
we can find a long, illustrious shelf of editorial minds
masquerading as architectural hands, whose collective efforts
came to define what we now think of as modern architectural
culture. Recall, for example, that Le Corbusier's very name
(today a registered trademark owned by the Fondation Le
Corbusier) was dreamt up by the architect in *l'Esprit nouveau*
as one of 14 or more editorial pseudonyms used during the
years that he reinvented the modern architectural journal
itself. Remember, too, Gropius's iron grip on the Bauhaus
in the 1920s, given voice and penetrating reach despite the
school's short lifetime, and made possible through his
unswerving editorial control of its publishing operations
located at the school's core. We can look elsewhere and find
Gerrit Rietveld's front-page editorials in *De Stijl*, which can
be looked back upon now as having played a much greater
role in spreading the missionary, modernist zeal of modern
European architecture than any of that architect's interior
decorating efforts. From all these little journals to the larger
professional magazines, modern architecture has been printed
much more than it has been built. As if further evidence
were needed of the editorial axis of architecture's twentieth-
century rotation, consider that even the verbally challenged
and textually reticent Mies – modernism's *sine qua non*
master builder – included as one of his formative
architectural experiences his short-lived leadership of the
little-known iconic architectural journal, *G*. Simply put,
red pens have long been the weapon of choice for rendering
architectural ideas (like its culture of expectations) modern.

Against the backdrop of this cultural lineage, *20/20* is
an invaluable compilation of the experiences and attitudes of

20 contemporary architectural editors whose activities speak louder than any of the words that follow (including, as any editor will tell you, those that have been deleted) regarding the ongoing project of forming architectural culture. As a volume it offers compelling evidence of the nuanced ways in which the legacy cited above has morphed in recent years into a more variable, expansive field of knowledge, aligning with a breadth of architectural experience that, like the media all around us, seems now in a constant state of flux.

The book confirms a wide range of editorial agendas that keep alive architecture's enduring belief in itself as a culture of ideas whose circulation and transmission remains of the utmost importance. Two immediate impressions emanate from the ink printed on its pages. Firstly, that editors continue to understand, indeed now take for granted (if rarely offered a space within which to voice) their vital role within architecture. Secondly, and somewhat unexpectedly in these early years of a new century supposed to be about something else entirely, architectural editing is enjoying a secret, largely unnoticed and nearly invisible, resurgence.

I say secret and unnoticed because of course we are all supposed to be living, 40 years after certain namby-pamby post-structuralists made exaggerated claims regarding the 'death of the author', in an era characterised by the mass extinction of mainstream print and publishing. Ours is a period more often than not characterised by its generalised assault on editorial (and not only architectural) intelligence. Such a view, like so many former proclamations of early deaths subtly amended by clear-thinking editors, is largely exaggerated. As a publisher and not only occasional editor and frequent writer of architectural words, I most certainly believe architecture editors are already enjoying a flourishing, at times even conspiratorial, underground. If not ample evidence, this book offers at least plenty of testimony of the breadth of this particular conspiracy theory (and one that works hard to contradict the contemporary master narrative of many accounts of contemporary culture).

In recent years everything from the world's great political scandals (the 'mis-information' used as a predicate for America's ill-fated invasion of Iraq), to the collapse of financial markets (the lack of 'proper' market reporting in print and television media outlets) has been blamed – somewhat bizarrely – as failures of editorial judgement. The US newspaper industry, in steady decline for the past 15 years, has seen its editorial staff slashed to a fraction of what it once was, while architectural presses, magazines and journals of all kinds have closed down alongside other specialist publications and bookshops as new media habits have taken hold. More threatening still to the modern, printed and edited architectural page has been the recent rise of new digital technologies that seem designed to make editors themselves redundant, as we have entered a new era in which everyone can now, at virtually no cost (or for most, editorial consequence) become their own worst broadcaster. In other words, in an age of Wordpress and wwwriting, when via a laptop or smart phone anyone anywhere can connect directly to a reader, why have editors at all?

I've taken my editor's advice here and slashed a couple of paragraphs that sought to rehearse the already well-worn lines of argumentation regarding the redundancy of the above question, the responses to which are starting to sound as increasingly flippant in 2010 as they did amid all that 90s bloggy hoo-hah we all had to endure at an earlier stage of battle. For evidence of the revenge inflicted upon those bloggers of architectural words who expect paper to be leaving architecture anytime soon, look no further than the 276 pages that follow, a first-ever contemporary compilation of architectural editing, both as a topic and book.

Paradoxically, one of the surprising consequences of the digital transformation of print and architectural

culture has been the secret rise of small presses, smart
editorial teams and tiny publishers working with a growing
generation of writers, which together have shown ways
in which small architectural publishers can thrive as niche
species within the larger, predatory open waters of mass
media production and culture. *20/20* is an embodiment
(not just a proclamation) of this reality. We at AA
Publications are indeed a small-time operation compared
to architecture's dominant publishing houses, but one that
shares with the participants of this book big ambitions
regarding the enduring reality of architecture as a form
of culture, communication and knowledge. In making this
project possible I thank Kirk Wooller for editing this volume
and bringing it to us so that it can in turn be brought to you,
and the wonderful 20 contemporary editors for taking time
from their busy lives and sharing their experiences. Of
course, even in the small world of architectural magazine
editing there could have been many other participants
who would have only strengthened our cause and expanded
upon the book's larger argument regarding the vitality
of architectural print today. In that magazines are by their
nature serial, we can look forward to the next volume as
a sequel, widening the conversation even further afield and
with it expanding upon the editorial, and therefore architectural, universe we know.

IMPOSSIBLE MISSION
Introduction by Kirk Wooller

The absurd logic of authoring a publication by editing other
editors hints at the entangled nature of how architects put
words to work. The decision to target editors from 20
polemical architectural magazines – however disguised these
polemics might at first appear – was an attempt to demystify
some of this absurdity by revealing the agency of editing in
architecture. A cynical reader may well be correct in thinking
that such agency generates a tacit pact amongst publishers
and the writings they facilitate. Indeed, besides the 'editorial
statement', the role that editors play in shaping architectural
magazines and the discourses they both enable and delimit
is a question seldom aired in public. *20/20: Editorial Takes on
Architectural Discourse* breaks this silence by providing an
open platform from which to elucidate editorial practice.
The aim is to bring together a myriad of contemporary voices
in order to provide today's architectural reader with concise
viewpoints from the editors behind the magazines behind
architectural culture.
      The somewhat naive idea of an 'open platform', how-
ever, signals the impossibility of this project. The naivety
stems not from the initial assumption that the editors themselves could submit a piece of writing that would not require
further editing. Nor does it result from the assumption that,
of all people, editors would adhere to a working deadline.
(Of course, editors know all too well the inherently flexible
system of deadline enforcement for non-periodical publications such as this.) Instead, the impossibility of an open
platform arises from the realisation that, although each
author may be willing to let their contribution stand 'as is',
inevitably these writings will pass through (in this case, four)

levels of (publisher) editorial control before the book reaches its audience. Such control constitutes various levels of influence, persuasion and refusal of material based on ambitions and agendas that remain concealed from public scrutiny.

Yet this scenario is by no means atypical. Consider for a moment, then, the possibility that the authorial ambition for this book is not so naive. If an open platform is deemed impossible, then what becomes possible when part of the editorial process is given an unusual degree of exposure? While this publication is certainly no investigative exposé of the particular workings of the editors involved, it is a *project* and as such is designed to achieve a particular objective: to place the editorial voices side by side so that adjacencies can trigger reactions in the readers, who will, of course, include the editors themselves.

The central criterion for selecting the contributors for this book results from an interest in the magazines they edit – publications that avoid promoting or pandering to the profession (realising full well that a blatant perpetuation of the status quo is often less dangerous than polemics that act as a subterfuge for similar ends). This has in no way left a collection of writers who preach only to their own converted. The range of editors in this book varies as widely as their publications' production and allegiances. Approximately half are in some way associated with academic institutions. The remainder are independent to greater or lesser degrees. Overall the magazines range in age from the oldest student-edited architectural journal in the United States (*Perspecta*) to one that (at the time of writing) is on the brink of being launched (*[bracket]*). However, most are less than 10 years old and originate from America, Britain, Continental Europe, Australia and New Zealand.

Each of the contributors has responded to a set of 20 questions. However, contrary to the popular quiz series 'Twenty Questions' – where the answer is predetermined and the players have 20 chances to guess it – the questions were not intended to reveal a particular answer. Instead, they were considered as 20 polemical prompts aimed at soliciting responses that begin to examine the conditions under which these questions come into being. Grouped into five loose categories, the questions target the justification, thematics, writing, institutions and culture of architectural publishing. With express instructions to consider these questions 'at will', each contributor was asked to respond to any or all (even ones left unsaid) that they saw as relevant to their own editorial work. The one stipulation was that each contribution should be specific to the editor's own endeavours and not some proclamation of 'the current state of...' As such, the project aims to provide insights into the multiple conditions under which particular ideas and words enter architectural discourse through publication – insights from the editors who craft the content that we read.

From the outset, the aim of elucidating these insights was not driven by an attempt to construct a set of tenuous threads between disparate opinions (a regrettably familiar endeavour that largely results in a feeble justification of sameness from difference). Such needlework serves only to justify a pluralistic position that rarely manages to agitate architectural conventions – a fundamental criterion for innovation. In fact, several of the publications were chosen precisely because their own editorial boards are placed in an intentional state of flux that avoids such reductive interpretations.

So why editing and why now? This publication is certainly not a response to claims that print media is suffering some form of slow demise, far from it. Despite over two decades of dire predictions, the book has not reached a state anywhere near resembling its 'death'. Likewise, similar warnings about the magazine have failed to come to fruition. If anything, the culture of the reader has managed to accommodate demand for both print and digital texts. Instead, we might do well to recall the words of Elizabeth Eisenstein, who wrote 'the more printed materials accumulate, the more we are inclined to overlook them in favour of more recent, less familiar media'.[1] While this was said in reference to the effects of the mid-fifteenth-century invention of the printing press, Eisenstein's words would inadvertently premise the creation of desktop publishing in the mid-1980s and the radical transformations this new technology would have on the publishing world. Indeed, her words continue to have currency today, when books and magazines are often eclipsed by digital modes of publication. True to Eisenstein's warning, alongside the current furore over digital publications that turn reader interest towards blogs, wikis, RSS feeds and e-books, a level of indifference has emerged towards the print magazine. As a result the publishers, editors and instigators of these magazines appear to exist in a public vacuum, devoid of the once-prevalent scrutiny of a reader whose interests now lie elsewhere.

The result of such indifference is the overlooking of the role that editors play in crafting the public arenas that enable scrutiny and critique. By definition and practice, editors shape and modify content for publication. In turn, architectural publications shape the way architects question their discipline's limitations and potential. Whether overtly or not, architectural editors empower the public arenas that their magazines create and in doing so frame architectural thinking to varying degrees. While most would not deny that editing is a process of inclusion/exclusion – perpetuating the stereotype that editors are the bane of a writer's existence – to keep the focus on this false opposition between an author's

1. Elizabeth Eisenstein, *The Printing Press as an Agent of Change: Communications and Cultural Transformations in Early-Modern Europe* (Cambridge: Cambridge University Press, 1979), p 17.

literary creation and its pragmatic restriction (the edit) comes at the expense of acknowledging editing as a creative, powerful and intrinsically political act.

In a 2003 interview with Susan Bell, Eliot Weinberger sheds light on a kind of editorial practice that holds true for a great deal of the architectural periodicals that adorn our libraries and bookshelves:

It's interesting that the word editor - in the American sense - does not exist in other languages. For example, the policy in Latin America with magazines is that you pretty much sink or swim according to what you write. They correct spelling mistakes and obvious things like that, but they pretty much publish it the way you wrote it. The result is that any given magazine has a much greater diversity of voices. [...] There's a greater diversity of quality, too, but there's a greater diversity of voices, unlike American magazines that all end up sounding as though they were written by the same person because the editor keeps rewriting the piece. Because they have a house style, everything gets poured into the mould. It doesn't matter what the subject is. Everything has to be in that beautifully polished prose. The editors sort of throw it into the Cuisinart and it all comes out sounding the same.[2]

This book, however, is neither a slight to editors nor a celebration of their virtuous yet unsung cause. The polemic is directed at the reader who fails to enquire into the editorial presence of what they read, as much as they might fail to edit their own response to the words, thoughts and agendas that inform architecture's discourses. As editing is a process

37

undertaken by both writer *and* reader – at a time when the interests of both seldom create any real form of public agitation – *20/20: Editorial Takes on Architectural Discourse* is a book that suggests the need for a more actively editing reader. As the longtime editor Susan Bell reminds us, 'the way we read, not just write, matters immensely'.[3]

2. Susan Bell, *The Artful Edit: On the Practice of Editing Yourself,*
(New York: WW Norton, 2007) p 38.
3. Ibid, p 211.

1. Do acts of criticality – beyond author selection or making better copy – validate your editorial work?

2. What enables you to determine a topic as worthy for public discussion?

3. If it is now almost effortless to become an author-editor-publisher of (at least your own) work, then does your publication offer anything more than another mode of personal opinion?

4. How do you determine the validity (or not) of the editorial statement?

5. Do the topics your magazine addresses question architects on problems that are yet to have defined solutions?

6. Can you avoid merely soliciting views on a subject about which your readers have an opinion already?

7. Do thematic issues generate new discussion or diluted commonality?

8. Are non-thematic issues polemically sterile?

9. Should there be a frivolousness to architectural writing, which confronts the seriousness of building?

10. Should there be a purposiveness to architectural writing, which confronts the whimsicality of opinion?

11. Does your publication need to exist through the instrumentality of an editor?

12. How does the format of your publication determine whether questions are considered productive or not?

13. Institutional publications traditionally exist as a means of disseminating scholarly work. Does your publication address the appropriateness of this system?

14. Are academics becoming more editor than teacher, more curator than creator?

15. How do architectural publications enable the pedagogical shifts that turn curricula into curated content, and what are the implications for this new architectural knowledge?

16. Does your editorial work examine the conditions under which both subject (author) and object (their field of enquiry) come into being?

17. In what ways does your publication critique the role of the architect in contemporary culture?

18. How do you defend the fields of enquiry that you, as editor(s), deem appropriate for architectural discourse?

19. Does your publication facilitate the sidestepping of traditional forms of scholarly architectural work in favour of more performative, design-based modes of criticism and research?

20. If so, then against what measure do you judge your attempts as being successful?

scapes

Number 4, Fall 2005

Department of Architecture,
Interior Design, and Lighting

PARSONS THE NEW SCHOOL FOR DESIGN

SCAPES

Silvia Kolbowski

In 2002 the Department of Architecture at Parsons School of Design in New York City asked faculty member Silvia Kolbowski to develop a journal for the department. Kolbowski was the editor of the resulting tabloid, Scapes, *from 2002 until 2005. Silvia is a time-based media artist whose works address the ethics and politics of history, culture, and the unconscious. She has collaborated with architects on multi-disciplinary projects and has taught widely in art and architecture programmes. From 1993 to 2000 she was a co-editor of* October, *and continues on their advisory board. In 2006 the editorship of* Scapes *passed to Joanna Merwood-Salisbury. Joanna is an architectural historian specialising in early modern American architecture and urbanism. She is Associate Chair of Architecture at Parsons. In August 2008 Joanna sat down with Silvia to talk about the origins and purpose of* Scapes.

Joanna Merwood-Salisbury: Maybe we can start generally by talking about the purpose of academic architecture journals. One of the questions we have been given to consider is, 'Does your magazine address problems that are yet to have defined solutions?' The answer to that would appear to be self-evident, but perhaps it isn't?

> Silvia Kolbowski: I think it is actually a good question. Many architecture critics at newspapers or monthly magazines focus only on personalities or recently finished buildings instead of focusing on more complex issues that have not been spotlighted.

JMS: They often see architecture as a branch of the fine arts, thinking of individual architects as 'artists'. That limits the way they can discuss the scope of architecture.

SK: This, of course, is also a problem in the general field of print journalism, where investigative journalism is rapidly disappearing. This seems to be why a new American website such as ProPublica has arisen, which was started by prominent journalists and editors, with the support of philanthropic money – to fill a gap. Why is investigative journalism disappearing? Is it the cost of dealing with globalisation? A drop in advertising revenue due to the expansion of internet businesses? The power of corporations to control what gets printed? Now, a small architecture journal doesn't face exactly the same issues, but that climate affects the field of architecture publishing, and small journals can be sites where different issues are addressed, or ignored.

JMS: I assume you're talking not just about academic issues but the ways in which architecture intersects with larger social, cultural and economic concerns. What does 'investigative journalism' mean in the context of architecture?

SK: At this point, it's more than obvious that architecture is implicated in many intersecting realms, including economics, politics and public health, not just aesthetics. But where do large American newspapers cover architecture? In the arts section. They could just as well cover it in news reports or in editorials, addressing the intertwining of architectural aesthetics and culture in a larger sense. The question is, who should be writing about it? Do you ask someone who knows a lot about real estate and city politics but doesn't know anything about architecture to cover the rebuilding of the World Trade Center, for example? How do you cover all the cultural, social, environmental and economic issues involved? Journalistic writing is – or should be – facing a huge crisis.

JMS: Do you think the architect's training makes him or her better able to address these issues than the journalist's training? Is this sociocultural awareness something that is already present in architectural training, or is it something we are still striving for? Architects may well be very aware of the complex relationships between formal objects and social issues, but they are not often well equipped to write about them, and they are not necessarily encouraged to write about them.

SK: I'm sure there are more than enough people who want to write about architecture! But even the field of architectural history, let alone architecture journalism, is relatively new. The older generation of critics and historians writing now were usually trained as architects. If you were to say to me, what degree would be essential for an architectural writer, I would say a studio degree in architecture. But obviously you have to have a facility for language as well.

JMS: Do you think that architectural education has changed to privilege writing more?

SK: I think some architecture schools now recognise the many different skills that architects need to have.

JMS: It is certainly true that the sort of writing that comes out of architecture schools is very different to the sort of writing that comes out of art history programmes.

SK: The difference is that an education in architecture is a professional education. You are taught a technical proficiency in the discipline, and studying history/theory or writing about it is peripheral, although crucial. That is very apparent to me having worked on the margins of architecture for 30 years.

JMS: I was going to ask you about that. Though we are both deeply involved in architectural education, neither of us is a practising architect: you are an artist and I am an architectural historian. How do you think our own practices have inflected the magazine?

SK: Before I was hired as the editor of *Scapes* I had been teaching at Parsons for several years, occupying a fairly unique position in having some knowledge about the relationships between art and architecture. That came out of the 80s when there was quite a bit of interaction, and sometimes collaboration between the two fields. In particular, architects and architecture students were quite interested in art and art theory, although it wasn't equally reciprocal.

JMS: Certainly that was a period in which artists were doing a lot more site investigation and had an interest in architectural and urban-scale production.

SK: A kind of second wave of site-related art. The problem was that it was too easy for architects and architecture students to collapse the two fields. The seminar I taught at Parsons ('Art and Architecture: A Parallactic View') was based on trying to get architecture students to understand the *differences* between art and architecture rather than the similarities, and that came out of seeing the rather

46

glib way that art was being instrumentalised in studios.
In other words, even though the '80s were a very
productive time for the overlap between the two fields,
I began to see the limitations of that interaction.

JMS: How did that influence the way you envisioned *Scapes*?

SK: Peter Wheelwright, the Chair of the department
at the time, asked me to coordinate public programmes
at Parsons and to start a journal. The goal was to give
the department more visibility, to bring in the public,
and to make the production of the department available
to a larger audience. But he gave me a lot of autonomy
about the definition of the journal. In formulating
Scapes, there were some basic conditions that I wanted
the journal to meet; I wanted it to include critical
writings on the challenges facing architectural practice,
a focus on issues of urgency in the world in which
architecture did or could play a role, and I was intent
on getting the students involved in the production at
least to some degree. In fact, it was through my
discussion with my first group of student interns that
we came up with the name *Scapes*. We considered the
title 'Interzones', but I think the allusion to William
Burroughs was inappropriate!

   Part of the idea of overlapping fields included
the decision to include an art project in every issue
that was somehow architecture-related, one that would
not feed into the desire on the part of some architects
and architecture students to fetishise or idealise art,
but rather to use art projects to expand definitions
of categories that were important to architecture, like
public space and urbanism for example.

JMS: In a similar way I have tried to include content that places contemporary issues in relation to historical concerns. For example there is a long history of valorising 'organism' in architecture that contemporary students aren't always conscious of when they talk about sustainability, although they are using many of the same terms and values. Maybe we can turn to the look of the magazine. What influenced its design?

SK: The original vertical design was based on the proportions of a famous Spanish magazine, *Arquitecturas Bis*, which had included a discourse of architecture that was broadly defined. I also wanted it to have the immediacy of a tabloid. At a very young age I worked at the Institute for Architecture and Urban Studies when the tabloid *Skyline* was started and I knew its first editor, so I might also have been influenced by the tabloid format of that journal as well.

JMS: What were your aims for *Scapes* when it first began? What kinds of topics and ideas did you hope to focus on? What was the relationship between the magazine and the institution that produced it?

SK: Something I felt strongly about, which Peter supported, was that we weren't going to produce something purely for show. So students were invited to participate because the journal was meant to stir up discussion amongst the student body as well as readers outside the department. It was part of the ethos of the department.

A lot of architecture departments produce publications that are completely divorced from the student body. Obviously there are exceptions like *Perspecta* where the students control the whole journal, which I think is quite remarkable. But I was absolutely deter-

48

mined not to produce a journal that was to the benefit only of the faculty. And the fact is that although Parsons students tend to be less trend-oriented and star-crazed, which is good, they can also sometimes be a bit detached from architectural discourse taking place outside their studios. So I always had a group of students involved with each issue. Some were engaged in the production work alone. But there was always a project that the students would handle on their own. I don't want to idealise it – it wasn't always easy for me as an editor to make demands on such young students to produce good research. I'm not sure that I ever achieved, due to studio time constraints placed on students, the quality of work I was aiming for. But I think that the process was always valuable to the students.

Maybe the best outcome was the timeline of Brazilian architecture that the students produced, because it managed to show the profound ideological implications of cross-disciplinary events. The timeline arose because they interviewed the visiting Jaime Lerner [the urbanist and former mayor of Curitiba], and I said to the students, how is Brazil able to develop these rather unique urban prototypes? There must be something in the genealogy of that country that allowed it to happen. That is why I asked them to look at architecture and urbanism in relation to political history, cultural history, urban history and Brazilian land rights laws. They did excellent research.

JMS: And that is an example of what you were talking about earlier, about placing architecture in its wider context. How much connection was there between what you saw happening in the school and the topics that you chose to address? Did you try to make up for a lack, or did you piggyback on what you saw was already going on?

SK: Well in a funny way I did both, because I was also the director of the public programmes at the department. The Michael Kalil lectures are one example [each year since 2002 the Michael Kalil Endowment for Smart Design has endowed a lecture series in memory of the designer at the Department of Architecture]. I worked with Jean Gardner, a longtime faculty member, to invite people for the Kalil lecture series to speak on extended issues surrounding architecture that we thought would either enhance the teaching at the school, or fill in some gaps, and we often interviewed that person in the journal, and represented their work. We had some architects and landscape architects, like William McDonough, Thomas Herzog and Julie Bargmann.

JMS: That tradition has continued with speakers like the environmental historian William Cronon and the community activist Majora Carter of Sustainable South Bronx. The Kalil certainly had a big impact on the department. For a while it was the defining association. It was ahead of the curve with the whole sustainability issue.

SK: It also introduced more global voices. And it was open to a broad public because we set them in the Joseph Urban-designed auditorium at the New School. One thing I wanted to do with *Scapes* and the public programmes in general was to be less New York-centric, less provincial, and to look at the wider world. I also made an effort to bring in people from other departments in the school. At that time there was a lot of talk about interdisciplinarity at Parsons and the New School but very little was actually put into motion.

JMS: That is something I wanted to ask you about, because the profound changes that have occurred in the school since

you started *Scapes* have been to do with the fact that it is
now very much focused on interdisciplinarity. The genesis
of this movement was when the former Provost Arjun
Appadurai began promoting interdisciplinarity as the
most promising way to align the various interests of Parsons
and the New School, particularly design and the social
sciences. While we have recently been through a period
of consolidation, the result has been to more closely align
the design disciplines, and unfortunately the social science
and liberal arts divisions of the university remain somewhat
isolated from us.

SK: In one issue we had a roundtable discussion on
interdisciplinarity between various faculty members
at Parsons and the New School. The reason I wanted
to do it was that it became apparent that there were
fields within the institution, but outside of design, that
we never interacted with: urban policy, the sciences,
international affairs. I wanted to know why there wasn't
more overlap.

JMS: What are the consequences of this emphasis on
interdisciplinarity for the magazine? Do you see it as
fundamentally an architecture journal that tries to
broaden our understanding of architecture by bringing in
conversations with other disciplines, or is this the moment
when it becomes a broader design journal that is not solely
focused on one practice?

SK: It was not my intention to broaden the focus
beyond architecture, although I wanted to consider
architecture in its broadest sense. If you look at the
table of contents you will see that while I did always
try to expand the boundaries, it was always with regard
to defining what is relevant to architecture. The

question is, what are the full responsibilities of architecture?

For example, I should explain how the 'Positions' series of articles in *Scapes* came about. The first issue of the now famous *Oppositions* magazine was a play on the idea of 'zero positions'. If you look at the cover of that issue you can see how that idea is graphically represented: the first 'p' is obscured. I don't fully understand what I think was Peter Eisenman's graphic play, which was later dropped, although I think it had to do with distancing *Oppositions* from concurrent ideological positions, or maybe all ideology? My inclusion of a series of 'Positions' articles was a play on that. *Scapes* was going to take positions. Unapologetically.

JMS: Why did you resign the editorship?

SK: Between 2002 and 2005 there were profound changes in the way architecture was being taught. There was a new attention to broader issues: urbanisation, land use, digital technology and globalisation. I couldn't remain an active artist *and* keep up with all these issues and do justice to them in the magazine. Probably the ideal editor is an independent editor who can keep track of all the issues and represent them in depth.

Log

FALL 2008
Aftershocks:
Generation(s)
since 1968

13
―
14

$15.00

LOG

Cynthia Davidson

In Gary Shteyngart's new novel *Super Sad True Love Story*, set some time in a plausible future of total dependency on personal handhelds, the character Lenny says, 'Reading is difficult. People just aren't meant to read anymore. We're in a post-literate age. You know, a visual age.' Shteyngart's riff on our new addiction to smart-phone technology may be prescient, but the visual age is already upon us. The magazine *Log: Observations on Architecture and the Contemporary City* was launched in 2003 precisely to resist the seductive power of media images through a format and content modelled on the literary magazine and the slow space of the printed page – on writing and reading.

    Log is the second magazine to be published under the umbrella of the Anyone Corporation, a nonprofit think tank founded by Arata Isozaki, Ignasi de Solà-Morales, Peter Eisenman and myself in 1990 to establish architecture as the host of a series of multidisciplinary conferences on the idea of architecture in a post-structuralist, undecidable context. The annual 'any' conferences, each held in a different international city and involving some 25 presenters over three days, were documented in books of the same name. To sustain discussions in the 12 months between meetings, in 1993 we launched *ANY* (or *Architecture New York*), a tabloid magazine that staged smaller public events in New York – such as 'Electrotecture: Architecture and the Electronic Future' (1993); 'Architecture and the Feminine: Mop-up Work' (1994), and 'How the Critic Sees' (1998) – and then reframed the discussions in its pages. Issues were thematic and usually developed in collaboration with invited guest editors, many of whom worked in disciplines other than architecture. In 1995, the Writing Architecture Series books, a collaboration of the Anyone project and MIT Press, was inaugurated with *Architecture as Metaphor* by Kojin Karatani, one of Japan's leading literary critics.

The heart of the Anyone project – its series of 'any' conferences – was designed to be finite; to end with the new millennium. The tenth and last conference, Anything, was held in 2000; *ANY* magazine ceased publication in October 2000 with number 27; the *Anything* book was published in 2001; and Elizabeth Grosz's *Architecture from the Outside: Essays on Virtual and Real Space*, also released in 2001, seemed to be the final Writing Architecture Series book. While the project was free of an institutional agenda, without institutional backing, funding was an endless task; raising money to support thinking (theory), rather than product (building), was next to impossible in the United States. After working literally as a volunteer for the last year of the project, I, with my board's approval, put the future of the Anyone project on hold. The price of institutional freedom had become too great.

Then the World Trade Center towers went down. When the dust had cleared and the fear had begun to subside, the discussion turned to architecture, to image, to memorial, to neighbourhood. Image dominated the conversation, particularly after the design ideas competition in late 2002. Those images seemed to preclude deeper discussions, deeper questions, about architecture and the city. Suddenly it seemed time to launch a new, but different, magazine, one no longer manifestly concerned with the graphic image, something other. The time for the big, bold, activating, thematic *ANY* had passed. Something like its opposite seemed necessary: a platform for interrogating architecture and a place where theory – which had become largely subsumed by 'research' – still had value. Hence, *Log* – small, contemplative and quietly subversive through critical 'observations' of contemporary discourse and building. There is the occasional thematic issue – such as 'A Critique of Sustainability' in *Log* 8, and 'Curating Architecture' in *Log* 20 – but these are pressing cultural and architectural matters, not simply concepts through which to look at architecture. By largely leaving *Log* open and unpredetermined, the opportunities for discovery and experiment, for mixing established voices with new ones, are more apparent.

As Beatriz Colomina thoroughly documented in the exhibition 'Clip, Stamp, Fold: The Radical Architecture of Little Magazines 196X – 197X', the magazine has had a critical role in advancing architectural ideas, and whole histories of movements can be traced in their pages. But if architecture today is ideologically (socially and politically) adrift, caught in a web of rapidly evolving technologies of design and production, and encumbered by media's fascination with celebrity, fashion and images, such 'radical' architecture magazines are nearly impossible. Instead, there are magazines that, rather than simply reflect the contemporary condition, question it; consider it with a critical eye; and, like Shteyngart himself, produce writing not to convey information but to convey ideas – writing for reading and the imagination.

Why reading in a largely visual discipline? In architecture, the drawing, or picture, is shorthand for representing ideas. These pictures are also iconic, registering a single image or idea as static and given. The ease with which one can insert a design proposal into a context through Photoshop produces images that in their slick clarity preclude questioning, even preclude the imagination; in fact, they may simply produce the kind of longing associated with consumer culture.

The old adage that 'a picture is worth a thousand words' can be read at least two ways: first, that the value of the image is greater than that of the word, or, second, that the image is more efficient than the word. These two interpretations alone illustrate the undecidability of words, the multiple meanings or interpretations of writing that can lead to new ideas – for example, that one 'word' – an algorithm – could today also produce a thousand images.

There are on average more than 55,000 words in an issue of *Log*, and 70 images – almost 1,000 words per drawing or photograph. With the exception of the occasional thematic issue, the writing is largely unsolicited, reflecting the ever-evolving views of the writer-architect more than the agenda of the editor. The editor's concern, my concern, is with producing a magazine of thought-provoking content: writing that surprises, that challenges, that analyses – but never simply informs. Through the selection and juxtaposition of texts, themes develop surreptitiously, cross-references occur, and space is made for a sustained discussion of contemporary issues in architecture that, out of desire, is printed on paper and bound between two covers.

Will this always be the case? Recently I came across an article about a group of friends who occasionally spend a weekend – 48 consecutive hours – making a 60-page magazine, called *Longshot*, simply because they like doing it. There was nothing in this article about content, only process. The editors solicited articles through Twitter and email announcements; they organised editing by using Submishmash and Google Docs; after layouts (with an unnamed software), copy editors 'scrubbed' the texts; and finally, *Longshot* was published at Magcloud, an on-line, print-on-demand service run by HP. It all sounded like something out of *Super Sad True Love Story*, except for the print-on-demand part. Why print pages of text if the handheld is king, or, as Lenny says, reading is difficult?

Reading can be difficult, in part because the perpetual distractions of information technology conspire to consume the time available for deep reading. Yet the Writing Architecture Series resumed publication in 2005, and we are now working on *Log* 21. For I would argue that one reads literature and architecture for the same reason: not for the story, not for the meaning, but for the writing itself. Pictures may remind us of our lived experiences; writing can take us beyond.

MANIFOLD 3
Winter, 2009 | The Interview Issue

MANIFOLD

Izabel Gass

Many descriptions of editors portray us as gatekeepers, allowing only certain content into the fortified institution of the academic publication. While a good editor plays this role to some extent, recent changes in the publishing industry and the state of architectural discourse demand a revision of this metaphor. Independent publishing, or publishing without the endorsement of a financially robust or academically reputable press, has become ubiquitous in the last five to ten years. In part, this is due to the proliferation of cost-effective alternatives to typesetting, such as online publishing and on-demand printing. But it is also symptomatic of a growing need for architectural publications to function less as trusted establishments that ensure the conventions of discourse and more as catalysts for exploding those conventions and allowing conversation to develop, unfettered. Today's editor is less a gatekeeper and more an instigator with an experimental impulse, guided by a discerning vision for the future of discourse.

With an understanding of this situation, *Manifold* was founded in an effort to address a void left in theoretical architectural writing following the cessation of the MIT Press journal *Assemblage*, the predominant forum for academic architectural discourse in the United States from its inception in October 1986 until its conclusion in April 2000. In the inaugural issue of *Assemblage*, its founding editor, K Michael Hays, had defined the journal as 'a format for oppositional knowledge – knowledge that continually questions received ideas, that challenges entrenched institutions and values, that strays from permissible terrain'. The intent of the journal was to question accepted architectural thought using the analytic tools of a broad range of intellectual developments outside of architecture, from Continental philosophy to science, from psychoanalysis to gender studies. The 'format for oppositional knowledge' provided by *Assemblage* was, by its very nature, an indeterminate one, yielding a plurality of articles. Yet, it was still a *format*: the journal imposed a discernible method for 'critical' academic writing on architectural discourse. Moreover, it was intended to circulate among a small group of readers who, for the most part, also constituted the publication's contributors, keeping its scope relatively narrow.

On the heels of *Assemblage*'s cessation, architecture saw the formation of a loosely unified 'post-critical' or 'projective' movement, constituted by a set of articles published from 2002 to the present, by authors such as Michael Speaks, RE Somol and Sarah Whiting, among others. While the individual views of these authors varied widely, all were in agreement that the *Assemblage* era for 'oppositional knowledge' had come and gone. In *A+U* (2002) Michael Speaks, arguably the most polemical among them, would argue 'theoretical vanguards were incapacitated by their own resolute negativity' insofar as they 'operated in a state of perpetual critique'.[1]

The post-critical movement struck a group of students and faculty at Rice University as inadequate to address the major questions confronting theoretical writing on architecture. Thus, *Manifold* was founded in 2007 as an independently funded, ad-hoc challenge to the deadlocked condition of architectural discourse. As we saw it, on the one hand, the *Assemblage* model for scholarly publishing had had a fruitful run, but had certainly run its course. It was time

1. Michael Speaks, 'Design Intelligence', *A+U* (December 2002), pp 10–18.

for architecture to override the oppositional 'format'. On the other hand, the growing anti-*Assemblage* backlash had merely generated a depressing range of uninteresting or, in some cases, simplistically anti-intellectual publications. In the spirit of a pamphlet intended for quick circulation more than an established journal, and funded entirely out of pocket, the first issue of *Manifold* included a smattering of book reviews, covering everything from John Rajchman's *Constructions* to Sylvia Lavin's *Crib Sheets*, and a few interviews, including one on the state of science and architecture with Sanford Kwinter and one on post-criticality with K Michael Hays. The theme for the issue was articulated as a question: 'What constitutes theory now?' But a polemical and dissatisfied undertone in the journal's content conveyed a more pointed message: architectural discourse had reached an impasse, and rigorous intellectual experimentation was needed.

Following the release of the first issue, the direction of our editorial work became clear. *Manifold* was a journal of architectural theory founded on the premise that philosophical enquiry and socio-political discussion had become increasingly marginalised since the decline of *Assemblage*. But, for *Manifold* to compensate for this lack without replicating the dead-end alternatives of architectural discourse present and past, the journal had to develop a self-critical capacity and abandon certain established conventions for journal production. To achieve this, we delineated three goals for the publication.

First, *Manifold* seeks to question what 'theory' is, what its ever-shifting value is and how it can be reconstituted to maintain its relevance to architecture today. Theorising architectural design in 2009 does not imply rehashing the same rhetoric characteristic of a previous era, but inventing the very tactics of criticism anew, and to invent anything anew is to take big risks. In editing *Manifold*, we have to be willing to supplant the editorial desire for reputable contributors and predictable articles with a willingness to take a chance on new names and experimental approaches. Moreover, *Manifold* does not restrict its content to topics obviously related to architecture, but surveys a broad range of contemporary intellectual developments. This does not represent the now common embrace of 'interdisciplinarity', which usually involves skimming the surface of other bodies of knowledge for metaphors relevant to building or design. In his 1979 *The Postmodern Condition*, Jean-François Lyotard noted that 'the idea of an interdisciplinary approach is specific to the age of ... hurried empiricism' in which the question that we ask of knowledge 'is no longer "Is it true?" but "What use is it?"'[2] Interdisciplinarity in architecture too often succumbs to this tendency of mining knowledge for its specific *utility* to design, which typically leads to superficial changes in the *representational strategies* rather than the *comprehensive conceptions* of architecture, because it adopts new knowledge in such a way so as to leave certain conditions of architectural production axiomatic and unchanging. This is evident, for instance, in design work utilising organic structures as formal models, or previous attempts to translate post-structural philosophy into spatial metaphors. *Manifold* instead seeks an understanding of the broader, contemporary episteme in which architecture is situated. By establishing an intellectual context for theoretical enquiry without forcing explicit connections between architecture and other forms of knowledge, we translate architecture's concern with form-making into an open-ended and potentially disruptive question: *How does one characterise space, form, thought and culture today?* The relevance of theory to architecture resides in its capacity to continually address this question with new answers.

2. Jean-François Lyotard, *The Postmodern Condition: A Report on Knowledge*, translated by Geoff Bennington and Brian Massumi (Minneapolis: University of Minnesota Press, 1984).

A second and associated goal for the journal is to thoroughly investigate the formal and philosophical principles of contemporary design through studies of extra-disciplinary source material that has been gutted in its current uptake by architecture. Over the last 20 years or so, architectural discourse has tended to freely appropriate terminology and metaphors from philosophy and the material sciences, transforming words that hold complex meanings within their original epistemological contexts into near meaningless buzzwords. Ultimately, this practice impedes both rigour and radicalism in thought because it substitutes real intellectual innovation for the use of vague descriptors and neologisms that neither reader nor author can fully define. The solution to the problem of empty jargon is not to dispense with it altogether, abandoning pioneering efforts to venture outside of architecture, but rather to press our own discipline to further extrapolate the meaning of the concepts we have adopted. This requires two editorial tenets: first, complex concepts should not be made more obscure through use of vague terminology; second, we need to direct enquiries towards a more thorough understanding of concepts and terms which have been accepted as commonplace, but which nonetheless remain opaque.

In issue 2, for instance, we chose to investigate the scientific and philosophical framework for terms such as the intensive, the virtual and the temporal. In the form of book reviews, we revisited the original writings of Albert Einstein, Gilles Deleuze and Henri Bergson to supply a more accurate and rigorous notion of what ontological immanentism might mean for the construction of the material subject, space and time – and consequently, for the foundational concerns of architecture itself. This presented a far more onerous but necessary engagement with material that had been otherwise neglected by contemporary design, but which had nonetheless come to inform its basic principles.

Our third goal is to develop, among our contributors and readers, a plurality of new voices and positions in the discussion of architecture. The post-critical (or projective) movement is, in many ways, a bit of an Oedipal struggle, an effort by one generation of theorists to 'kill the father' or oust an older guard of writers. This is an inevitable consequence of the limited number of dominant voices in the conversation on architecture – myopic, internecine struggles often take the place of open communication. Publishing has historically supported this tendency, allowing the same small set of well-known authors to dominate a single periodical. *Manifold* aims to break with this tendency.

Our third issue, 'The Interview Issue', epitomises this effort. It includes 14 interviews on topics ranging from predictable architectural themes such as landscape urbanism to more esoteric concepts, like atheistic theology (Mark C Taylor) and aesthetic ecstasy (Philip Wood), to broader questions about the state of cultural theory, such as the political role of the academic (Eric Lott). This diversity of material was enabled by the interview format, which presents an opportunity to break from established conventions for academic discourse, soliciting more pointed, rhetorical or intimate reflections from interviewees. In an age when sound bites and synopses have supplanted sustained conversation in the mass media and elsewhere, the formal interview creates a welcome opportunity for focused conversation in which interlocutors can hold one another accountable for clarifying thoughts and statements, or to engage in debate. We have slowly learned that the editorial work involved in generating good interviews is not in modifying them after completion, which often stilts the tone of the conversation, but in establishing a basic framework for the interview and then allowing the conversation to freely develop from there. A good interview will always betray the interviewee's impulse to communicate – the need to catalyse a discussion then follow its implications, to come to know and share an idea through structured dialogue.

This impulse to communicate in fact characterises *Manifold* and distinguishes it from other, more established publications. Like an eager conversationalist, *Manifold* seeks to discuss what has been left unsaid by these publications. It speaks to and with a wide range of contributors and readers, motivating an engagement in architecture and thought in general. In that, *Manifold* offers a model for publication that is less like writing and more like speech, addressing very contemporary and specific topics of concern and responding to the state of ideas instead of reinforcing entrenched scholarly conventions. *Manifold* has less intention of becoming an institution *itself* than of pressing for radicalism within the existing institutions of architecture, as enabled by its status as an independently published journal produced with complete editorial freedom.

Manifold has largely avoided affiliation with the forms of authority, regulation and institutionalisation that do nothing but undercut a spirit of intellectual experimentation, and is not edited in such a way so as to enforce a 'format' or a 'template' for publishing. From one issue to the next, *Manifold* shifts its tone, its graphic layout and its conceptual focus as necessary. Our mission is not to enforce consistency in each issue of the journal but to invent fresh forms of presentation that challenge architectural discourse to explain itself. We have not sought affiliation with a distributor because we do not want uniformity and brand recognition imposed on the publication. This, of course, leads to a loss of academic legitimacy, but that loss is less significant for us than the editorial freedom gained. *Manifold*'s editorial model represents what we foresee as one robust avenue for publishing in the twenty-first century, characterised by provocation, risk-taking and experimentation, both unrestricted and unrestrictive in its scope, but rigorous in its methods.

MARK

MARK Nº 25
APRIL . MAY 10

—————— ANOTHER ARCHITECTURE ——————

Ceci n'est pas une maison

MARK

Arthur Wortmann

Just another day in April 2008 at the *Mark* editorial offices.
In the morning we get confirmation that 13,600 copies of
Mark #13 have been shipped from our distribution centre on
an industrial estate in Capelle aan den IJssel, a stone's throw
from Rotterdam, to subscribers in 74 countries and bookshops in 55 countries. In that issue, 48 completed buildings
from 12 different countries are featured and discussed. In the
afternoon an invitation from the Architectural Association
lands on our digital doormat: would *Mark* like to contribute
to a book about 'the current state of architectural discourse'?
We must be doing something right, we think, when a little
magazine gets invited to participate in something like that.
In the evening there is a match in the Champions League of
European football: Liverpool-Arsenal. A British get-together?
Not really. In Liverpool's starting line-up, under Spanish
coach Benitez, we find three Englishmen; in Arsenal's, under
the Frenchman Wenger, not one. This is an apt illustration
of the global society in which we live – a situation that also
defines the way we look at architecture.

The first issue of *Mark* was published in September
2005. When we were working out the plans for the new
magazine, three principles were key from the very beginning.
The first was a radically international perspective. While
virtually every self-respecting architecture journal has
adopted the predicate 'international' by now, there is almost
always a clearly identifiable national home base. Sometimes
they are even lumbered with being bilingual. We felt that
a new periodical, without connections to a local institution,

without the ballast of a tradition, without obligations toward a subsidy provider, would be able to focus, carefree, on the Champions League of contemporary architecture, the playground of international transfers and worldwide distribution of images. Was this not in fact a logical step, in an era when some architects spend more time in airplanes than in their offices, when no training programme is complete without an internship or a masters abroad, when the internet ensures that hypes cross the oceans instantaneously? The frame of reference of the architect in the twenty-first century has become completely global.

Our second principle has always been that we wanted to view the magazine as a visual medium. *Mark* is the sister publication of *Frame*, an interior and design magazine launched in 1997. By 2005, eight years of *Frame* had taught us that the designer audience is visually oriented. It is okay to read (in fact it is necessary) but a magazine should first seduce and enchant. The visual intelligence of today's reader is so great that pictures can say more than a thousand words. As the Swiss architect and visualiser Philipp Schaerer remarks in an interview in *Mark* #15, the excursions to the holy places of architecture history that were once obligatory for the training of an architect are increasingly a thing of the past: by now we are capable of drawing conclusions from well-produced and well-presented visual material. There are likely to be few architecture periodicals in which the image is as cherished as it is in *Mark*. Literally every image is optimised by the editors, designers and lithographer based in Amsterdam. That too is a result of globalisation: either you opt for the financial advantage of production in low-wage countries, or you benefit from the increasing service and quality that ought to be a differentiating factor for the enterprises in the local graphics industry.

Graphic design is also part of a visually attractive magazine. Over the last several years, architecture has unmistakably acquired a fashionable component. The surface can no longer be dismissed as superficial; it contains a whole range of subtle meanings. That interplay had to have an effect on the medium. The jury of the European Design Awards 2008, who delighted us with the first prize in the magazine category, characterises Lesley Moore's design as follows: '*Mark*'s ever-changing design expresses contemporary architecture's fluid, rapidly changing nature, and also its obsession with form, "skin" and texture. It does so through graphic experimentation, bold use of photography and an original approach to typography: each issue displays a custom-made typeface, based on one of the three typefaces – Futura, Goudy and Gridnik – used throughout the magazine. Its simple but sophisticated layout manages to explore clearly identifiable themes, while respecting photography and the projects it showcases. A truly twenty-first-century magazine.' Naturally, we could not have put it better ourselves. The prize did not stop us from moving on, however. A growing reputation and an increase in circulation (as 2010 comes to a close, we're at 19,000 and counting) led to our adoption, in December 2008, of a slightly more sophisticated and mature design. *Mark*'s new graphic designer, Mainstudio, was promptly awarded a Golden Cube by the New York-based Art Directors Club.

The third principle is the attempt to escape jargon and academicism. In *Mark* we wanted direct communication. We are not conducting science; we are not a podium for the products of 'industrialised architecture theory', as Brett Steele called it in an interview in *Mark* #11, the highly personal output of researchers lost in their own niches. We are curious: we want to uncover the motivations of architects and use them to inspire. There is probably no international architecture journal with a higher proportion of interviews than *Mark*. This anti-academicism is not anti-intellectualism. The best evidence of this is perhaps our approach to the book section, which in many periodicals has an obligatory character. In *Mark* there are no reviews, but every issue includes a lengthy conversation with a theorist or designer about his or her favourite literature.

Mark is not associated with any institution, cultural or otherwise, and it is not part of a large publishing concern. *Mark* and its sister magazine *Frame* are led by an editor-in-chief and a publisher who started the company together, along with a small club of people they have collected around them. Besides editors, this includes a distributor, advertising buyers and subscription administrators. The lines of production could not be shorter. All critical information in a single pair of hands means optimal service, flexibility and a natural cross-pollination between the commercial and content aspects – a far more satisfying situation than the usual tug-of-war between parties with divergent interests.

The choice of an editorial staff to offer a radically international perspective naturally means setting up and maintaining an extensive network of informants and correspondents. The editorial office is like the palace of Kublai Khan, receiving messages from a hundred Marco Polos (might *Mark*'s last name be O'Polo?) simultaneously exploring the empire of contemporary architecture and – quite differently from the Tartars 700 years ago – bringing back reports with the speed of a fibre-optic network in text and images.

Information requires editing. Initiatives like that of worldarchitecture.org to build a global community with an infinite number of participants and projects are not very useful. Without selection, a platform with a steady readership and a certain amount of interpretation and direction, information is powerless. Projects can inspire, but they do not do so on their own. The choice of photographers, the selection of photographs, the format of the publication, the organisation of the information, and the tone of the text:

all of these contribute to make a project communicate. The work of the editors consists of doing full justice to a project by placing judicious emphasis on certain aspects.

At the *Mark* lunch table we seldom talk about things like 'facilitating the assimilation of criticality', 'new mandates for design' or 'digital technologies of quantitative and qualitative performance-based simulation to offer a comprehensive approach to the design of the built environment' – pronouncements that can be heard in certain circles of architecture criticism. If you wanted to lay it on thick you could say that each issue of *Mark* contains a bundle of love letters, stories about beautiful things. That does not mean that the shortcomings of these transitory contacts are not sometimes acutely laid bare, or that bafflement and disbelief never outflank admiration, but *Mark* is first and foremost fascinated by what is going on and by what architects have come up with. In that sense *Mark*'s role is no different from that of other architecture periodicals: it is the antechamber of historiography. The way it performs this role, we think, is what sets us apart.

Translation: InOtherWords, Pierre Bouvier

FOOTPRINT   DELFT SCHOOL OF DESIGN JOURNAL

TRANS-DISCIPLINARY
AUTUMN 2007

FOOTPRINT

Tahl Kaminer & Lukasz Stanek

Footprint *is a peer-reviewed academic journal focused on architectural research and theory. Founded by doctoral candidates at the Delft University of Technology and inaugurated in October 2007,* Footprint *has so far published six thematic issues investigating architecture and the city. They include* Trans-disciplinary, Mapping Urban Complexity in an Asian Context, Architecture and Phenomenology, Agency in Architecture, Metropolitan Form, Digitally-Driven Architecture *and the forthcoming seventh issue on* Drawing Theory. *In order to strengthen the relationship between the journal and research, each issue is edited by a different team of editors, focusing on a topic directly related to their own expertise.* Footprint *is published periodically – twice a year, in spring and autumn – and is available for free in electronic files on the journal's website, and for purchase in hardcopy. The main decisions are taken by the editorial board, which appoints new editorial teams, decides upon the topics of forthcoming issues and oversees the process of publication and peer-review. The advisory board of* Footprint *controls quality and offers advice and suggestions concerning the long-term development of the journal.*

This Is Not An Academic Text

To call a journal *academic* is hardly complimentary under the reign of coolness in today's architecture discourse; this is particularly true in post-1968 architectural academia for which a self-renouncement forms the foundation myth. Embracing the new roles assumed by the architect – including that of advisor, mediator, specialist in public space, curator or cultural producer – and eager to get a share in these exciting opportunities, much of academia pursues rather than questions these changes. Whereas the celebration of the post-1968 utopias goes hand in hand with the boastful rejection of marxism, the increasing pressure on researchers in European universities to establish cooperations beyond academia in order to generate external funding appears to be a timely pretext to outsource the responsibility for choosing the object of research, and provides an opportunity to prove that the architectural academia is finally doing something 'useful'. This situation is not ameliorated by the criteria of the natural sciences becoming again the yardstick for all academic performance, which inevitably compromises architectural research and its syncretic methodologies borrowed from art history, social sciences, technological studies and philosophy. Consequently, with its financing made possible by the current stage of the institutionalisation of architectural research within academia, *Footprint* aims at redefining architecture research from within.

Postulating *Footprint* as an academic journal necessarily implies a critique of much of today's academia. *Academic* signifies for us a position which is critical and self-critical; historically self-aware; ready to question the criteria of objectivity; committed to long-term engagement rather than 'hopping' between short-lived projects; based on deliberative rather than institutional criteria of quality; and refusing to substitute issues of fund-raising and international visibility for content-based criteria. Being academic also implies a community based on friendship – that is to say a possibility of disagreement. For this reason the journal is edited by a rotating and constantly growing group of academics rather than run by a closed circle united by a single career strategy;

and its aim is to operate only by issuing open calls for papers rather than individual invitations. This is facilitated by the journal's use of the internet: the free distribution of online files makes the journal widely accessible; such accessibility, in turn, is important in the context of severe budget cuts in universities and schools of architecture, many of which are too small to afford multiple subscriptions to journals, whether paper-based or electronic.

Academic means also a concern for the question of disciplinarity, understood as a means of generating criteria of quality specific to the research in question; disciplinarity is a precondition for allowing architecture research to address pressing and current social questions. Against the rhetoric of hybridity and the marginality of architecture discourse today, *Footprint* does not operate in the interstices but aims at the disciplinary centre, a centre which manifests itself as a void in today's debates. The definition of this centre cannot be carried out by a branding gesture or by copyrighting novel terminology; instead, there has to be a persistent commitment to research – empirical, historical and theoretical. *Footprint* pursues this research by taking architecture and the city as its point of departure and subjecting the core themes and methodologies of each issue to a constant debate by the issue's editors and the editorial board. These themes and methodologies are developed by an unfolding of positions, concepts and questions that define the debates in architectural culture in a longer perspective, rather than by *a priori* definitions or by submitting to current 'hot topics'.

Academic also means being curious about various scientific cultures, sensitivities and discourses, rather than succumbing to the hegemony of Anglo-Saxon research. Since most of the editors of *Footprint* follow research published in English, French and German, an awareness of the limited – and often marginal and full of misunderstandings – exchanges between these grand traditions inform the foundation of the journal. Thus, from the very beginning our intention was to include European perspectives in the global debate on architectural research, while accepting English as the language of the journal: not only because we all speak it at *Footprint*, but also because it is *not* the mother tongue of any of us. This diversity of perspectives was initiated already in the first issue, which included contributions from scholars who work in very different languages and research cultures.

Rebuking academia is the conventional 'rebellion' of twentieth-century architecture, from Le Corbusier's attacks on the Beaux-Arts to Koolhaas's mocking of academics while being a professor at Harvard. As we have never been academic, it is time for something new.

Architecture   Art
Media   Politics

Grey Room
40

$18.00

GREY ROOM

Reinhold Martin

I must first note that I do not write on behalf of the editors of *Grey Room*. I only write as one editor among five, on the basis of my own experiences working on the journal, which have run alongside other activities that also engage a number of issues addressed by the questions. Furthermore, where the questions seem to presuppose a relatively stable discipline, *Grey Room* does not. Thus the makeup of its editorial group; thus also the contents of a typical issue. Architecture represents only part of the journal's scope (and audience) and even then it relates mainly to how that discipline intersects with others. This is not meant to imply that *Grey Room* is only secondarily concerned with architecture. On the contrary, I would suggest that this kind of liminality, this relational character, is what defines the discipline itself and renders it constitutively unstable. In this respect, I think that one important contribution the *Grey Room* project has been able to make to architectural discourse has been to suggest that the techniques of 'media archaeology' (or archaeologies of media) offer a productive means of historicising, analysing and evaluating the status of architecture as one among many media.

This can mean many things, but it does not mean technological determinism, nor does it mean merely analogising architecture to mass media formats. It means thinking through the problem of media/medium at the formal, technological and socio-political registers simultaneously. I do not think that *Grey Room* has by any means adequately summarised the problem. But we have tried to open it up with respect to the history of architecture and art, and the many discursive arenas within which these cultural forms are produced.

So the short answer to the questions is that what matters is content, not format. Yes, we consciously opted for the format of the printed academic quarterly, with thematic issues as a relative rarity but a regular publication rhythm as a necessity. Like all formats, ours has both inherent possibilities and limitations. And it seems equally clear that, despite the care with which each individual issue is edited, designed and produced, many of our readers (especially students) read the journal in a piecemeal manner rather than one issue at a time, downloading PDFs from their academic library's online subscription portal rather than reading the physical volume at home or in the reading room.

I mention media archaeology because that subject, which by its nature overlaps with or includes a number of disciplines, represents a possible name for one of the many intellectual interests that may guide a *Grey Room* reader through their online search. To the extent that this accurately describes (in part) both the intentions and the actuality of the journal, many of the questions you pose here change their meaning. The reader may or may not be an architect or an architectural scholar, and they may or may not encounter specifically architectural material in their search, but I am fairly confident that they will encounter ideas and subjects that impinge directly on their understanding of architecture. It is not obvious what it means to suggest that architecture be understood as one among many media (a formulation that is my own, and not an editorial statement). It is only obvious that this proposition, or something very much like it, needs urgently to be addressed by any field of enquiry that has felt compelled to use words like 'technology' or 'computer' or 'software' (or 'design', for that matter) as ritualistic incantations that magically endow a rather confused discourse with contemporary relevance and meaning.

In that sense, I do wonder whether it makes sense today to refer to architecture as a discipline in the traditional sense at all. In many ways disciplines, like professions, are artefacts of the nineteenth century and can be shown to correspond to specific media regimes, specific ways of organising and disseminating knowledge and specific reading publics. Can anyone credibly identify architecture's 'reading public' today, whether in a specialised or a general sense? Conversely, what do (or should) architects read if they have time to read at all? My example of the hypothetical *Grey Room* reader searching for articles on or around the subject of media archaeology suggests that, as a member of a somewhat heterogeneous and diffuse readership, she may or may not consider herself to belong to the discipline called 'architecture'. But I sincerely hope that she will learn something about architecture nonetheless.

THE YALE ARCHITECTURAL JOURNAL

PERSPECTA 38

ARCHITECTURE AFTER ALL

DEBATE
MEANING
THEORY
JUNKSPACE
CONSENSUS
IRONY
PRACTICE
OPPOSITIONS
LANGUAGE
BILBAO
PEDAGOGY
9/11
MODERNISM
URBANISM
1968
HOLLAND
FEMINISM
CLASSICISM
FORM
BLOB
GLOBALIZATION
POST-MODERNISM
IMAGE
FASHION
AUTONOMY
NARRATIVE
SIGNATURE
TECHNOLOGY
MARXISM
IDEOLOGY
INTERNET
TRADITION
SUBURB

PERSPECTA

Marcus Carter &
Christopher Marcinkoski

Theorem: a theoretical proposition, statement, or formula embodying something to be <u>proved</u> from other propositions or formulas.[1]

Theory: a proposed explanation whose status is still <u>conjectural</u>, in contrast to well-established propositions that are regarded as reporting matters of actual fact.[2]

In response to the thematic outlined by the editor of this publication, this essay attempts to situate writing as only one component of contemporary architectural production rather than as an autonomous, self-driven discipline. In this model, writing exists alongside design, teaching, lecturing, experimentation, prototyping and publishing, as complementary pursuits that generate bodies of knowledge and create instrumental feedback reinforcing the architectural project.

We were asked to contribute to this publication because of our roles as editors of an issue of *Perspecta – The Yale Architectural Journal*. Conceptualised in Spring 2003 and ultimately published in early 2006 (#38 for those of you searching on Amazon), this issue of *Perspecta* attempted to document a selection of particular modes of practice we as editors felt were emerging in the early years of the twenty-

1. http://dictionary.reference.com/browse/theorem
2. http://dictionary.reference.com/browse/theory

first century. As we outlined the editorial structure for *Perspecta* 38, we imagined this great thing called Architecture – really the intersection of architectural thought and production (ie, building) – that could only be understood through processing the multitude of fragmented positions enabled by years of disciplinary production. We weren't interested in advocating a singular position because in the end any ideological stand remains relative to any other, and can therefore always be defended with the right lingo. Today more than ever, it is painfully clear that the 'one and only' solution of generations past is simply neither a professionally viable nor intellectually sustainable approach to architectural production in the twenty-first century.

There is little disagreement on our part that the relationship between the practice of architecture and writing on/about/for architecture manifests itself under various modes of operation, thereby achieving varying degrees of accomplishment. Many of these yields can be highly fertile and productive documents capable of generating an expanded expertise around a particular subject or agenda (think MVRDV's *FARMAX*). Other products of the architecture/writing nexus have demonstrated an increasingly disturbing self-promotion and self-reference that is a bit like watching a drunkard or addict slowly tear himself down via the very cocktail that made him so much fun to be around in the first place.[3]

Rather than wasting our breath promoting a singular ideology, we sought to cut what we termed cross sections through the discipline to dissect the issue as it related to

3. At that moment of editorial conception, the godfather of late-twentieth-century American architectural theory compelled us by claiming his own martyrdom. Peter Eisenman a few years earlier had claimed architectural theory to be dead, and who were we to argue with him? The 'post-critical' as a designation seemed horribly anticlimactic, so we thought at the very least we could try to claim naming rights to the next big thing…whatever that turned out to be!

the larger whole. By introducing the prefix 'after' before each topic, we hoped to provoke the selected authors to simultaneously glance back while projecting ahead to future trajectories. Themes such as globalisation, theory, pedagogy, form, image and ideology among others filled out the list. We viewed these 'agendas' – for lack of a better term – as indicative of a new pluralism manifesting itself in an emerging era of 'anything goes'. The architecture discipline at this point seemed to be driven by a strikingly refreshing sense of optimism, existing in a happy state of coexistence brought on by the supposed omnipresent potential of digital production and technological innovation – and let us also not forget the (seemingly now lost) benefits of a healthy economy.

Problematically, we as editors, without intentionally doing so, perpetuated a particular species of architectural theory even as we endeavoured to scrutinise it. Two years later, the writing of this very essay demands what seems like super-human strength to resist the draw of delving back into vague and now corrupt topics such as criticality, autonomy and authorship. The attempt to debunk critical theory and the institutions that support it by citing new modes of 'critical' operation simply made us complicit to the whole ruse. Fortunately, we can find comfort in the fact that we still have our day jobs.

In any case, others had already attempted to drive the stake in the heart of critical theory (or at least reframe its dominance) much earlier than we could have hoped for. *Assemblage* 41 comes to mind – especially the essays by Michael Speaks and Robert Somol – but so too does the *Oppositions Reader*, K Michael Hays' *Architectural Theory Since 1968*, and the slightly late to the game *[Re] Reading Perspecta*, among others.[4]

Yet despite all of this inherent potential swirling around the architectural ether, many academics here in the States stubbornly refuse to accept that ideas of concept, rigour, experimentation and intellectual engagement need not rely on critical theory to constitute a legitimate scholarly pursuit, and those that do, likely remain over-burdened by its very association. One can sense an obvious shift in the way that young architects are practising – combining design, teaching, writing and research to form a new definition of praxis that is entrepreneurial, optimistic and projective, as opposed to a previous model that was closed-minded, unduly critical, overly self-referential and ultimately self-defeating. We (of this generation) have all been fed a hefty dose of critical theory in school and for the most part have chosen alternative routes. It is clear that this swerve illustrates a greater interest in design and practice with the clear and immediate intention of contributing to the built environment, rather than engaging in the egregious insularity of the critical theory project.

Innovation Through Research

Love your experiments (as you would an ugly child). Joy is the engine of growth. Exploit the liberty in casting your work as beautiful experiments, iterations, attempts, trials, and errors. Take the long view and allow yourself the fun of failure every day. – Bruce Mau

In the hope of being consistent with our original position, we have chosen here to outline characteristics of an alternative mode of praxis rather than attempting to define a singular ideological position. Under this scenario, we view architectural production as a multidimensional approach in which trajectories such as building, writing, experimentation, teaching, testing, prototyping, etcetera form a matrix of praxis that is capable of privileging particular dimensions based upon an evaluation of given circumstances. This mode of praxis mines and exploits real conditions – both material and immaterial – to uncover opportunities rather than projecting unrelated complexities onto a particular situation. Looking outside the profession allows one to uncover innovative solutions to analogous situations, thereby enriching and broadening the consequences of a particular project. Certain aspects may come to the fore, but at no point does the model completely abandon the other dimensions of the matrix in favour of a singular trajectory. At a fundamental level, the basis of this mode of operation centres upon the simple notion of research – an architectural equivalent of the common notion of investigation in the context of rigorous academic pursuits:

Research: the diligent and systematic enquiry or investigation into a subject in order to discover or revise facts, theories, applications, etc.[5]

Though this definition is familiar to the point of seeming benign, two terms within the description are fundamental to our characterisation of architectural research as an alternative mode of praxis. The first term of significance is revise. The importance of revision lies in the fact that it

4. *Assemblage* 41 was ironically the only issue of *Assemblage* that either of us felt compelled to purchase – up to that point, photocopies of particular articles seemed adequate. There was something striking about it as a document – it was an end that seemed comfortable in its own finality, almost optimistic, even if it was a bit short on specifics of how to proceed. It read like a toast at a wake. Fittingly situated between Robert Somol and Sarah Whiting, Eisenman's essay read like he was making the last stand at the gates for the autonomy/criticality position that he, above anyone else, forced upon the discipline. What made the whole scenario even more entertaining was that neither Somol nor Whiting hesitated to give the old dog one last kick while he was down. Talk about oppositions!
5. http://dictionary.reference.com/browse/research

suggests that a particular fact or position will not remain fixed for eternity, but can evolve and change over time as additional information becomes available or if existing information is disproved. This idea of revision applies at both the strategic and tactical levels. Within the metaphor of research, the concept of strategy functions as the hypothesis or concept at the base of an experiment. The tactical aspect involves the actual physical form of the element(s) deployed and instrumentalised to provide a particular design solution that offers flexibility and suppleness rather than a singular, fixed solution.[6] This of course provides a striking contrast to the limiting ideological rigidity of previous periods within the history of architectural production, most notably modernism and postmodernism – and its peculiar cousin, critical theory – where the surrounding discourse was less about the pragmatics of the solution than the ideological position it 'represented'. Within the research-based practice, the notion of revision necessitates that the architect must play the role of editor in the culling of information; the iterative mode of the design practice; and the final definition of a design solution, as well as what that solution ultimately prioritises. We premise this definition with the idea that the architect continuously evaluates the design based on performance in relation to programmatic, urban and social parameters that define the criteria by which the iterative process is assessed.

The second and perhaps more important notion that resides in this definition of research is the concept of

6. An example of this kind of approach can be found in James Corner/Field Operations High Line project in New York City. The strategic aspect involves a stated desire to retain the found-condition quality of the existing elevated rail structure. That hypothesis translates into a tactical approach of using a robust system of planking and seating that allows for limitless variations in how hard and soft surfaces, as well as planted and public areas are composed and choreographed in relation to the existing structure.

application. Important here is the idea that enquiry, investigations, theories, etc can – upon the occasion of an opportunity – be deployed in practical endeavours that allow for objective testing of a particular intellectual trajectory. Research-based praxis allows for the emergence of empirical evidence and for the objective evaluation of a position by all parties, and not just the author of a particular approach. This kind of hyper-pragmatism allows for a new sense of entrepreneurialism in architectural production that moves the architect away from the secondary role of service professional back to the primary position of director or executive.[7]

Scientists and engineers remain more highly valued socially and professionally than architects because their role can be measured in the patois of efficiency and efficacy. These disciplines are respected for their broad contributions to society, rather than their local contributions to a particular discipline. Three decades of self-aggrandisement have left the American architect, in particular, lost at sea. We believe a return to empirical research, as the basis of praxis, will enable a re-expansion of the contemporary role of the architect.

This position should not be read as an advocacy of standardisation or the flattening of design; we see quite the opposite. The research-based praxis not only positions itself upon the objective input of various parameters, but at the same time acknowledges the subjective input of the author

7. The social and cultural relevance of the architect diminished substantially during the 1970s, 80s and 90s (particularly in the US) due in large part to the profession's supposed intellectual leaders' embrace of critical theory and abandonment of basic tenants of functionalism and professional responsibility. Long gone are the days when government agencies like the Department of Defence or successful (at the time) global corporations like General Motors would call upon an architect like Eero Saarinen or Louis Kahn to provide expertise in helping them to define a strategic long-term vision. The optimistic potential of architecture has been replaced by the pessimistic commodification of the profession for stylistic or branding opportunities. Planners and politicians are now in charge of defining the make-up of our collective built environment. Architects on the other hand are now relegated to drawing up someone else's 'big' ideas.

in guiding this curatorial process. We believe research should help one comprehend and exploit the externalities affecting design while opening up new trajectories for exploration. Enabled by the rapid advancement in digital communication technologies, the dissemination, examination and application of research have become easier and occur in an expanding variety of means.

To demonstrate this potential, we see five broad, overlapping areas – though not an exhaustive list – under which research can reassert the relevance of the architect: technique, materiality, expanded context, urbanism, and organisation/interface. Work within these areas aids the agile praxis driven by an expanding intelligence that coalesces through enquiry and experimentation. We suggest suppleness as a way of operating rather than as a purely formal or material characteristic. The research-based approach consumes information and conditions, mines it for opportunities, and then turns pragmatics over to find design opportunities. It treats complexities and restrictions as advantageous circumstances, not obstacles. Architectural production evolves into a process of experiments and feedback loops, constantly recalibrating the work of the architect to the real (as opposed to formal) parameters of a given condition.

I. Technique

Technology is increasingly driving the development of design and prototyping techniques in contemporary work. The best utilisations of new techniques avoid the pitfalls of formalism to create work with performative objectives. To be sure, we favour technology as only a means to an end, not as the work's *raison d'être*. Now that we have had time to get over the novelty of software and prototyping, we must think of these as mere tools added to the arsenal. Technique can empower the designer by creating a more direct link between design and production. As such, research into other fields of production – such as automotive design or industrial design – might suggest new ways of building that can circumnavigate the limitations of an archaic construction industry. Most examples to date remain in smaller projects, but the potential exists for mass-customisation on an increasingly larger scale. Harnessing new technologies has also allowed smaller offices to begin competing in the same arena as more established firms. Networking, prototyping and scripting enable smaller practices to innovate, not through an *a priori* theoretical position, but through experimentation that creates a continuous feedback loop that informs the research. A telling moment occurs when you first open SHoP's website to read 'Use technology to build practice, see practice as technology'. The firm innovatively merges technology, design and the financial parameters of a project in the conceptualisation and construction of their work. The Camera Obscura project in Greenport, NY in particular provides an example of a small research-based design solution in which SHoP was able to construct the building entirely from digitally fabricated components.

II. Materiality

Technology has allowed architects to rediscover materiality and at the same time push the limits of these materials. Unlike the immateriality of many modern projects or the paper architecture that followed, a renewed focus on tactility brings this contemporary work in touch with those who actually use it rather than letting the project fester as only an abstract idea or image within a book or magazine. The disappointment in the work of many of the so-called digital architects is that the realisation ends up mimicking the appearance of the computer simulation – ie, plastic. A few of those who are pushing the envelope – literally – have found surface and skin to be a fertile ground for experimentation in materiality, where the building's facade becomes performative and has a new sense of pragmatic ornament. The emergence of a practice like Front Inc, a boutique facade consulting firm in New York, illustrates a collaborative model in which the consultant brings technical expertise coupled with a strong design sensibility to the table. Similar to Cecil Balmond's contribution to many of the more structurally ambitious projects that have recently been published, Front brings about another form of knowledge that aids the architect in realising complex skins in projects such as OMA's Seattle Public Library, Herzog & de Meuron's Walker Art Center, or SANAA's Glass Pavilion.

III. Expanded Context

Globalisation did not occur overnight but one can unquestionably say it has arrived and has radically shifted our notions of context. An expanded context looks beyond just scale and form – though they remain factors – to engage the less tangible but no less critical elements that come into design. Politics, economics and, above all, cultural issues provide parameters and specificities that the designer should understand and utilise in his or her work. Contextualism becomes less about picking matching wallpaper and aligning window lines, and more about navigating and instrumentalising cultural, social, political and economic nuances. The broader understanding of context also speaks to the issues of duration, movement and virtual space, concepts that may not seem 'architectural' but in fact do intersect with and shape our physical imprint. This research into expanded contexts has produced a number of 'architectural' publications that have less to do with specific architectural products than with an architectural context. These publications represent the hypothesis or strategic approach by a practice or architect outlined earlier. Due in large part to their quasi-analytic tone, they are often more intellectually compelling and provocative than the projects they ultimately produce. Rem Koolhaas' Harvard Project on the City series and the recent *Volume 12: Al Manakh* illustrate some of the more obvious examples of recent contextual research driving architectural production. The increasingly pervasive blog also illustrates the expanded context of publishing enabled by technology. Democratic and non-elitist compared to, say, the old New York boys' club that put out books like *The Charlottesville Tapes*, these blogs enable the broad dissemination of opinions with varying degrees of anonymity, and thereby little accountability.[8]

IV. Urbanism

Along with globalisation and the information age, we have witnessed the rapid urbanisation of many parts of the world that once depended primarily on agrarian economies. This has brought about an expanded role for the architect in which scale and complexity multiplies beyond that found in a single building or city block. These projects require a very different type of knowledge and process than that employed in smaller

8. *The Charlottesville Tapes* represents the transcript of a not-so-publicised conference at the University of Virginia School of Architecture in 1982 with a 'who's who' crowd from a particular generation. Those privileged to be invited presented current projects and then were subjected to discussion and criticism by the others around the table. This was followed up by a second similarly organised conference/publication titled *The Chicago Tapes*. Despite the oppositions voiced with each of these settings, the ultimate goal of these 'conferences' was to further the ideological agenda of all those fortunate enough to be present.

projects despite what some architects believe. To avoid the mere importation of normative western models of urbanism to new contexts, a cataloguing and analysis of different systems of organisation needs to occur. The Dutch – in large part due to their unique terrestrial conditions – have spearheaded research in new urban organisations. Publications, many quite large, have emerged as an important part of this research process. A book like *FARMAX* or *KM3* exists as the product of urban research of MVRDV but should not be seen as an end product. The information contained in these tomes can be mined to inform individual design decisions as well as anticipate further research trajectories.

V. Organisation & Interface

Attention to the organisation and interface of programmatic and/or occupational adjacencies can produce new and unexpected spatial conditions and physical environments. Just like certain material qualities, strategic programme manipulations can become performative aspects of a project. This also challenges notions of normative use patterns independent of, yet coexistent to image or form. Many exclaimed that architecture could no longer relate to the user, that it had become an autonomous entity, indifferently coexisting alongside us. We believe that a renewed efficacy can and is already occurring in many recent projects. This flies in the face of both games of autonomy and notions of pure efficiency. Organisation and interface speak to the utility and effect a project has on us whether we are cognizant of the way the building changes our relationship to the city or how the materiality or light in a particular space can alter our particular disposition. Work AC's PS1 installation, Public Farm 1, provides a striking example of an urban intervention that subverts easy formalism to operate on multiple levels, even operating as a narrative text with its didactic lessons of urban ecology. Situated within an otherwise barren concrete courtyard, it simultaneously provides shelter for the hipsters, encourages participation in an exhibition on urban farming, and supplies much needed greenery to this slice of the Queens concrete jungle. At the same time it provides vocation for prison workers at Rikers Island who are responsible for supplying the planting content. This installation demonstrates the potential, at multiple levels of utility, which can be exploited and juxtaposed to create a compelling degree of conceptual depth within a single project.

Let's Get To Work

Genius is one per cent inspiration and ninety-nine per cent perspiration. - Thomas Edison

In contrast to work of another period, architects today must refuse to become bogged down in the superfluity of theory. As such, innovation can now occur through an expanded definition of practice through building, writing, experimentation and teaching all under the veil of research – with the ultimate goal of substantive contributions to the built environment. This illustrates a new optimism and entrepreneurial attitude that looks to engage the complexities of the system – instrumentalising them from within – rather than standing against it from the outside lobbing criticisms. Lying somewhere in between theory and formalism, the informed and performative project provides direction towards a new intellectual model.

The acquisition of intelligence through research is not intended to cast the architect as expert. Rather, collaboration both within and (in particular) beyond the discipline is an essential component of this model. It enables the architect to pool resources but also exposes him or her to non-architectural expertise related to the built environment such as culture, politics and economics. Collaboration also serves to promote dialogue within the practice that intentionally subverts the notion of a singular dominant style or position. This places the architect as an active agent in the process and development of the built environment rather than as a critic whose only role is commentary after the fact. Rather than discourse for discourse's sake, research both informs the product and exists as production itself, creating feedback within the design process. Writing and publishing must exist only as a component of this process, not an autonomous discipline competing for the attention and resources of the non-architectural world. The self-referentiality of critical theory and autonomous formalism has only served to weaken the profession of architecture within the global political and economic reality. It is only by becoming projective and entrepreneurial in its modes of production that the architectural profession can bring an end to its self-imposed isolation and actually engage in productive interdisciplinary work that will expand a body of expertise and its disciplinary role rather than just continuing to talk about it. Research-based praxis aims to reunite conceptualisation with realisation.

The model of praxis we are advocating here is certainly not new. The process operates on the familiar if/then model in which the result of each step informs the position of the next rather than promoting a wilfully ignorant predetermined trajectory in which the steps remain the same regardless of the specific circumstances of the project. Rather than imposing something that is conceptually alien, the research-based approach endeavours to mine the given conditions of a project to produce solutions with greater robustness and flexibility. It is both optimistic and opportunistic.

Ultimately the intention of the research-based practice is to promote an agile, supple model of praxis responsive to

106

the complexities of building in the early twenty-first century. Future intellectual leaders of our discipline must expand the role of the profession through productive speculation. Only then can this refocusing position the architect as an active central agent in guiding the broader definition of the built environment rather than simply a service professional carrying out someone else's charge.

As they say, the proof is in the pudding...

Tijdschrift voor Architectuur / Architectural Journal

OASE #69

Posities
Positions

Gedeelde
Shared

gebieden
territories

in histo-
in Histori-

riografie
ography

& ontwerp-
& Practice

praktijk

OASE

Christoph Grafe & Johan Lagae

As far as journals for architecture are concerned *OASE* is a fairly exceptional publication. Founded by a group of students at the architecture faculty at TU Delft in 1981, *OASE* is made by a collective without a chief editor (not even a *primus inter pares*). It covers articles of a length now only found in specifically academic publications and the topics raised in each issue can be so wide-ranging as to defeat attempts at categorising them or discerning an editorial line. If anything, *OASE* is a product of a particular intellectual culture emerging from the 1970s that would combine an interest in the rigorous analysis of architecture's cultural, economic and social contexts with a study of the formal and compositional questions of design as a cultural practice. The early editors of *OASE* were certainly acquainted with *Oppositions* and its combination of academic seriousness with a selection of topics that primarily originated in the individual fascinations of the editors or contributors. This was, and continues to be, the guiding principle of *OASE*: a journal made by academics and practitioners (usually with some academic connection), who use the journal as a vehicle to pursue their interests and intuitions of architecture as part of a larger culture.

Academia and Practice

OASE may appear as a magazine of a 'both … and' kind: *both* publishing texts that are the result of academic research, which are subjected to a process of peer-review and are

111

published without concessions to assumed attention spans of practising architects, *and* articles that transgress the boundaries of academic propriety by being either overtly literary or speculative, *and* texts documenting architectural projects. This format, which has become rare amongst architectural publications, allows us to address questions about the relationship between design practice, criticism, history, theory and the role of architecture as a cultural practice. It also implies a particular position vis-à-vis the divisions of labour which have emerged in the field since the 1970s, between a practice that has increasingly adopted a pragmatic attitude towards its own modes of operation (and its history) and an academisation of theory, which proposes itself as a critical court of appeal but often tacitly accepts the separation of making architecture from thinking about it (if not explicitly sanctioning architectural practice).

Possibly a more precise description of the position of *OASE* within the current typology of architectural publications – from professional magazines that document current production to scholarly journals that operate as an outlet for academic research – is that of 'neither'.[1] What is important is not that *OASE* publishes different kinds of contributions resulting from the catholic taste of its editors, but rather that the journal's openness towards various formats and types of argument creates a space for critical reflection that allows both editors and contributors to step outside the disciplinary confines of their particular milieu, be it academia or practice. For the editors, there is a deliberate choice to use the medium of the journal to invite alternative modes of critical reflection on the current conditions governing the field of architectural publications.

1. This position of 'neither' was first coined by Marc Schoonderbeek and Filip Geerts, who were key to the production of the anniversary issue *OASE #75. 25 Years of Critical Reflection on Architecture*, 2008.

The Themed Issue as a 'Project'

In this respect the format of the themed issue is crucial to
OASE's *modus operandi* as well as for the position we try
to occupy in architectural culture. While the editorial board
of *OASE* functions as a collective, it does not work according
to a consensus model; the format of themed issues thus offers
a way of managing the variety of interests and divergent
views on architecture held by individual editors. The recent
practice of also working with guest editors has been significant in adding new voices to the body of ideas, convictions
and approaches that already exists within *OASE*. This is
reflected in the range of themes of the recent issues: architecture and literature, historiography, the public domain,
and invention.

The themed issue is crucial for occupying the position
of 'neither' since it provides a particular opportunity to open
up space, in terms of both quantity and quality, in order
to develop intellectual projects. Indeed, the themed issue
provides a particular and rare intellectual space to 'test' the
discursive practices and conventions of both practice and
academe, in which both *OASE*'s editors and its contributors
normally operate. The fact that individual editors have a large
degree of freedom to define the concept for a themed issue,
and the presence of both practitioners and academics in each
of the groups editing a particular issue, is essential here. Each
themed issue is an 'architectural project' with its own logic
and character as an experiment in self-education, for which
no preconceived format exists. An *OASE* issue can contain
the more classical genre of long articles or project
documentations as well as more intricate (possibly frivolous)
ones, such as free-wheeling literary impressions, (staged)
dialogues and conversations or visual essays. Crucial for every
issue is how these different formats and genres interrelate and
work together to construct a reflection on the chosen theme.

The role of the larger editorial board, then, is to serve as a sounding-board for developing arguments. The graphic design, by Karel Martens and the *Werkplaats Typografie* in Arnhem, also plays an essential role in the project, as it is always conceived in dialogue with the editors of a particular issue, so that it is attuned to the concept and form. The restraint and focus on the legibility of the graphic design distinguishes *OASE* from other magazines and lends the journal an overall coherence, notwithstanding the variety of topics addressed over the years.

Slowness

As an intellectual project which is neither a classic magazine nor a book, the themed issue provides a territory for an in-depth reflection on a specific topic, the slowness of which contrasts with the inevitable immediacy of architectural criticism in professional journals. *OASE* cultivates a position of restraint towards the (assumedly inevitable) rapid and fundamental evolution of both architectural practice and discourse, while also deliberately steering away from the smoothness that characterises, in both content and form, a large part of current publications and debates. We have followed, for instance, the emergence of Dutch architecture in the 1990s and its international branding as 'Super-Dutch' from a fairly studied distance. If the choice of topics *OASE* addresses is steered by the desire to be relevant to current practices and discourses, in particular in the context of the Low Countries, we do maintain a preference for a certain slowness that informs the selection of topics. In all its diversity, the themes addressed in *OASE* betray an adherence to the *longue durée* of the architectural discipline. This historical perspective remains key to the agenda of *OASE*, even if this perspective tends to be confined to the twentieth century and, even more particularly, to the postwar period.

History and Criticality

The current debate about the necessity or desirability of a critical stance in architecture and its publications suffers from a tendency towards abstraction. Architectural writing – if it is aware of the historical perspectives and particular circumstances surrounding each position (in practice as well as in academia) – cannot avoid being critical. But this is not to say that history in *OASE* is intended to be operative for contemporary architectural practice, similar to the writings of those figures Anthony Vidler recently labelled 'historians of the immediate present'. Nor does it mean that history in *OASE* is confined to its own disciplinary boundaries, as is the case with more strictly academic publications. Rather, it provides a looking glass through which to discover ways in which architects, critics and others operate within the conditions of their time, in order to understand mechanisms at play in the production of the built environment that may still be relevant today. By combining a historical and a critical method with an in-depth analysis of particular buildings, starting from the idea that each building or project demands its own critical approach, this method demonstrates our belief that the historical perspective is significant for critically assessing current practice. Or, put differently, 'history matters'.[2] As such, the role of history in *OASE* comes close to that of a select group of journals that have now all but disappeared (one might think here in particular of *Oppositions, Daidalos, Archithese*, but also *Arch+*).

2. Alice T Friedman, 'History Matters', *Harvard Design Magazine*, Winter/Spring 1999, pp 53–58.

Local Internationalism

As a journal, *OASE* intrinsically links to the local contexts in which it operates. Originally founded as a student magazine at the TU Delft, it is now hosted by NAi Publishers in Rotterdam. Given the personal and institutional links with the Netherlands and Flanders, *OASE* describes itself as an architectural journal rooted in the Low Countries. It is from this perspective that architecture is examined. There is an element of cultural resistance in this: architectural questions are often directly connected to cultural and political developments and, as such, they almost always have a local context. This emphasis on the local goes against the tendency of many architectural publications which depict architecture as an instrument of global branding, the celebration of icons, or the instrumentalisation of architecture for realising the market value of certain physical environments (cities or regions). In a way, the self-imposed local character of *OASE* (expressed also in our retention of a local national language alongside English) also implies a position on criticality: if architecture is discussed in its context, then this inevitably means a critical and precise examination of the performance of buildings or projects in social and cultural terms.

At the same time, this critical reflection is part of a wider context. The fact that *OASE* operates in a relatively small European region (with a long tradition of receiving, disseminating and publishing ideas in other languages) allows us to register discourses in various cultural and linguistic traditions. The heterogeneity of the editorial board reflects this tradition, with members coming from various backgrounds and territories (beyond the strict confines of the Low Countries) and operating within extensive, but not necessarily overlapping, international networks. The issues the journal produces, then, not only highlight some of the particularities of the local academic and professional scene but also seek to address a wider international audience. In this sense *OASE* has acquired the role of an intermediary between the professional and academic discourses in different (mostly European) countries. But through a deliberate choice to continue publishing in Dutch, we strongly wish to contribute to the local architectural culture. As demonstrated by the work of Geert Bekaert, one of the most original and profound architectural thinkers based in Flanders, developing an architectural culture in the Low Countries also implies subscribing to the challenge of finding the right Dutch words to speak about architecture.[3]

A Privileged But Fragile Position

We believe that architecture is a rich and complex field of cultural production and knowledge that continuously redefines itself *vis-à-vis* spatial, societal and cultural challenges. Critical thinking and writing on this role of architecture, both as a force of change and as a mode of reflection, is considered to be the main project of *OASE*. There is a certain fragility to this, and as editors we choose to protect this characteristic against all sorts of pressures from publishers, academia, professionals or subsidising bodies. These continuing efforts and struggles are fed by an acknowledgement of the privileged opportunity of working in such a 'neither' space. *OASE* is the result not only of a labour of love but also of a conviction that, against the background of an increasingly globalised practice of producing architecture, the kind of open intellectual space the magazine offers to us, its editors, is an opportunity to be cherished.

3. On Bekaert, whose first writings on architecture date from 1950, see the impressive ongoing publication project *Geert Bekaert. Verzamelde Opstellen* (editors Christophe Van Gerrewey & Mil De Kooning), the seventh volume of which was published in 2009 (in total eight volumes are planned).

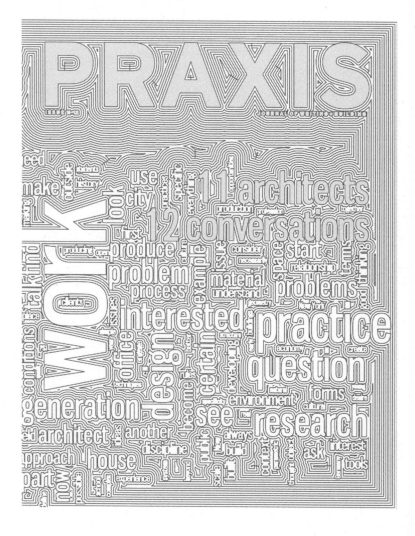

119

PRAXIS

Amanda Reeser Lawrence

Praxis, too, began with questions – in our case five rather
than 20. We printed them in the editorial of our first issue,
'Architecture + the University', nearly 10 years ago, as a
provocation and an inaugural framework for the journal:

1. How does an architectural project engage ideas or link
    concepts and actualisation?

2. How can architecture be conceived not as a commodity,
    but as a solution to a programmatic, spatial, urban or
    material problem?

3. What architectural practices are overlooked or under-
    represented by the mainstream architectural press?

4. What characteristics are shared by various architectures
    of the Americas?

5. How are transformations in cultural, social and economic
    paradigms affecting contemporary practice?

These five questions articulate a series of issues and interests
that continue to drive how we select material and frame each
issue. But they also define a broader editorial strategy.
Questioning necessitates a certain flexibility and agility. It
refuses a singular or dogmatic agenda. Since the responses
are often surprising, questioning requires an openness to
unplanned directions, to swerves and tangents. Beginning

with questions implies a loss of control. Of course, questions are also always leading. They preclude certain answers and suggest others. They demarcate areas of interest and reveal the bias of the interrogator. And questioning implies a dialogue, or some kind of two-way exchange.

For us, then, this open-ended and yet imperative nature of the question, the simultaneously connotative and denotative quality, was a particularly apt place to begin. More precisely, beginning with five questions defined a dialogical framework suited to our original interest: the relationship between theory and practice in architecture.

When Ashley Schafer and I founded *Praxis* in 1999, we began with the relatively simple idea of bridging the gap between trade magazines and academic journals. If each of these genres seemed to isolate certain aspects of architectural production and discourse – an uncritical and often superficial presentation of largely built work in the case of the former, and a highly theoretical discussion, almost entirely detached from architectural production in the latter – we believed that a hybrid publication could capitalise on the strengths of both. Importantly, this arose from a conviction that such a connection already existed within the field, that a relationship between academic and professional cultures was in fact being actively explored on both sides of the fence. In other words, we didn't set out to create a relationship between theory and practice but rather to offer a place to publish the proof of its existence.

At the most basic level, we achieve this by publishing both theoretical, text-based essays and highly detailed, image-based documentation of architectural projects, built and unbuilt. Whenever possible we try to include the writing and building of the same architect. This is intended not simply to invite correlation by the fact of their juxtapositon, but rather to provide a basis for interpretation, allowing for an evaluation of each according to the other. A kind of self-imposed criticality is inherent in this pairing: the thesis of an argument is only as valid as its appearance in the work. Including both an architect's writing and building also reinforces our position that architectural writing is simply a different manifestation of architectural practice.

This theory/practice connection is reinforced through the issue thematic. Recent examples have included architecture's relationship to capitalism, the role of technology, the concept of programme and an investigation of surface. While they engage the theoretical, these thematics are resolutely grounded in the design and making of the built object. The issue thematic emerges from identifying current trends in architectural practice and discourse, and the projects in each issue are chosen based on their engagement with the theme, but there is also a feedback loop whereby the thematic is reconfigured and readjusted according to the chosen projects. This 'testing' offers a kind of internal proof and ultimately a fortification of the theme.

The framing device of the thematic allows for alignments and groupings which might not be immediately or obviously apparent in the work. It enables us to create new connections rather than simply reinforce existing ones, and sometimes even to break down preconceived ones. In our 2004 'Landscapes' issue, for example, we identified a burgeoning trend within architectural practices to co-opt landscape methodologies. Architects had begun to use the concepts inherent in landscape architects: to think in terms of the logics of flows and flux, of indeterminacy, and to recognise the importance of time, contingency and issues of sustainability. Through a series of projects and essays we explored precisely how architects were making connections with landscape; in a relatively straightforward example, we published the only comprehensive documentation of the Fresh Kills competition, a landmark competition in which teams of architects, landscape architects and urbanists generated collaborative solutions for how to reprogramme the former landfill site for Manhattan. The framework of the issue, however, also allowed us to reinterpret projects that *wouldn't* typically be understood as landscape. Our feature on Diller + Scofidio's Blur building on Lake Neufchatel, created for the Swiss Expo in 2002, for example, challenged its interpretation as a sublime technology or whimsical folly. Instead we reframed the project as a landscape – more specifically a technological landscape. This interpretation opened up a more precise reading of the project in terms of its connection to the lake and the importance of the instability and ever changing nature of the 'cloud'.

Through the thematic, then, a deliberate and decisive collection of projects and articles coalesces around a common idea. Mitigating the inherently arbitrary nature of editorial selection, the theme becomes an active participant in establishing the questions that we ask of each project and text – not the least of which is 'should we include it?' Rather than questioning whether we find a project compelling, or interesting, or any other string of purely subjective evaluations, we instead ask ourselves whether the thematic – surface or programme or technology, etc – is the driver behind the design and, if so, how we can make that evident through our publication.

For an architect to edit a magazine... is a way of cultivating theoretical reflections, not as a separate activity, but as an indispensable part of design craft. – Vittorio Gregotti

Gregotti's insistence on the connection between theoretical reflection and the design craft was particularly resonant as we began the journal, and continues to inform how we conceptualise it today. The way we create each issue of *Praxis* is deeply rooted in the techniques and methods of the architect. *Praxis* is our practice.

The organisational structure of the journal is set up like a small architectural office or atelier, with two 'principal' editors and a series of six to eight revolving project editors, all of whom are practising architects. We work on a pin-up and review basis in all of our editorial meetings. Project editors carry each article from the publishing analogues of schematic design through construction administration: assembling the material, selecting images and drawings, working with the contributor, writing and/or editing text, designing the layout, writing the captions. The deep understanding of the material enabled by such an approach, and the lack of a centralised editorial control, generates a multiplicity of voices and graphic formats. This organisational structure was an early and significant decision, aimed at dismantling the instrumentality of one or two principal editors and replacing it instead with a community of editors, necessitating a more collaborative approach. Our editorial position thus emerges from a discursive field rather than a proclamatory agenda of a single editor. This format also allows each article to achieve an independent criticality *vis-à-vis* the issue thematic and the remainder of the articles, since it is effectively an autonomous entity within the overall issue.

This understanding of *Praxis* as a form of practice carries through to the design of the object itself. While every magazine or journal is necessarily designed to a greater or lesser degree, the design of *Praxis* is fundamental to the journal's editorial position. Each issue is a collaborative design project. Though we operate with a template, there is no standard layout. An editorial intent drives every design and layout decision: What drawing type and format would best reinforce the article's thesis? Is colour necessary to understand design intent? Would a text-based or image-based article better represent an author's position? Should an interview with the architect be included? Should we feature multiple projects from a firm to better understand their agenda?

The most significant illustration of the primacy of design in our conceptualisation and framing of the journal are the issue covers. We see each cover as an opportunity not simply to feature a selected project, as is typical in trade publications, or even to illustrate the idea behind the issue as a whole, but instead as an integral contribution to the conceptualisation and framing of the issue. Each cover represents an exhaustive, collaborative design process in which we ask ourselves/explore how we might perform the issue thematic through the design of the cover: in other words, how the cover might advance the issue thematic rather than simply represent it.

The cover of the landscape issue, for example, featured a pixelated image of the Blur building, printed on a second electrostatic sheet layered over the cover, reinforcing the editorial position that landscape had become a 'thickened' and layered condition. A sense of depth was further achieved by allowing a series of terms from the table of contents to telescope through to the cover, introducing another layer of information and further reinforcing its dimensionality – in this case a connection to the contents of the journal and its conceptual position. In our fifth issue, 'Architecture after Capitalism', we explored the relationship of architecture to contemporary economic culture. How could the cover engage issues of capitalist production? Through an investigation into the waste generated by the offset printing process, we arrived at a solution in which the 'overprints – test prints run through the printer until they're so saturated with ink that they're no longer legible and are then discarded – were reappropriated and reused as the cover. Our only intervention was to foil stamp the *Praxis* masthead in gold or silver. And in issue 6, 'New Technologies://New Architectures', our investigation into innovative technologies in architectural production was carried over into the technology of printing itself: the cover image was printed in thermochromic ink, which disappears when heated above a certain temperature. When a reader grabs the journal the image disappears and the table of contents is revealed beneath. In each of these examples the cover was developed as a design project, and evaluated using the same criterion with which we evaluate the projects within.

Each issue of *Praxis* is thus a designed object as well as an analytical and interpretive tool for theorising a body of design work. Our intention is not to provide an outside or somehow 'neutral' critique of architectural culture but an active engagement with it. Our deliberate embededness within the terms and tools of architectural practice challenges the distance traditionally sought by the critic or historian and instead proposes a decidedly operative editorial voice. In this way, we aim to connect theory and practice not only within the pages of the journal but in how we design and create each issue.

AAfiles

57

AA FILES

Thomas Weaver

The psychotherapist Adam Phillips once wrote that 'Psychoanalysis does not need any more abstruse or sentimental
abstractions – any new paradigms or radical revisions – it
just needs more good sentences.' This, in essence, sums up
my relationship to architecture and architectural editing. The
journal that I edit is, I hope, distinguished by the quality of
its sentences. I like pacey, engaging and iconoclastic writing,
essays rather than papers, and an almost indulgent use of any
form of reference. I really don't like the words 'commonality',
'instrumentality' and worst of all 'criticality'. But, compelled
by this questionnaire, before I launch into my own private
manifesto and risk more first-person narrative than is
absolutely necessary, a few salient details.

   AA Files was launched in the autumn of 1981 as the
successor to a long line of Architectural Association School
of Architecture house journals that began in 1887 with *AA
Notes*. It was founded by the AA's then chairman Alvin
Boyarsky, with Mary Wall as editor. In his introduction to the
first issue, Boyarsky suggests that the ambition of the journal
is to offer a more accessible engagement with the culture of
the school than the 'club-like' AA premises in Bedford Square
(its origin, therefore, seems to have been empowered with
correcting an architectural failing). He defined this
accessibility as the publication of AA lectures, reviews of
AA exhibitions and profiles of AA staff and student projects.
Over the ensuing 29 years and 61 issues, just as successive
directors of the AA have had to manage the weight of
expectation in succeeding the charismatic Boyarsky, so too

have *AA Files* editors had to deal with school directors who, like Boyarsky, fancy themselves as editors. There have been three directors post Boyarsky and three *AA Files* editors, all of whom have ultimately worked through relationships at turns supportive and confrontational. Part of the problem is that the AA is both a school (an open academic institution) and an association (a closed members' club) – although this characterisation itself can be inverted (the school is private and open only to those who can pay its fees, and the club, for a modest subscription, is open to anyone). The journal, then, has long had a competing agenda – to try and promote the introverted world of the association while simultaneously trying to engage and celebrate, more expansively, the wider subject of architecture. (Although this too can easily be subverted – what the association considers as architectural culture is often more accommodating than the particular stylistic, technical or methodological allegiances propagated by the school.) The politics of this relationship between architecture and the AA's publications is infinitely more exhausting than any actual editing.

Beyond the historical and cultural context of *AA Files*, however, what these questions on editing architecture seem to be asking, above all others, concerns the ability to establish some sense of quality. Words like 'critical', 'valid', 'appropriate' and 'successful' are all, in effect, synonyms for a standard you hope to achieve. No editor of a journal would ever aspire to publication that wasn't good, but the problem, for me, comes when the abstraction of the synonym is used to defend the legitimacy of the endeavour – does Kenneth Frampton's *A Critical History of Architecture* really offer a critical history because he brands it as such? I realise that the cult of criticality is an easy target here but it is still so prevalent. No month of my working year goes by without a proposal for a critical essay, practice, project or exhibition. The counter-position, however, is equally hazardous. At a recent AA lecture Peter

Cook declared that 'architectural discussion has been hijacked by people who call themselves architectural theorists' and that 'the efforts of teachers and other intellectuals to divert young architects' interest away from things to abstracts have been pernicious and so needs to be redressed'. Tiptoeing between an over-entitled theoretical obscurantism and a literalism that denies the importance of anything other than the physical object is endlessly difficult, but at least the flow of architects and architectural thinkers passing through the AA offers some kind of respite. To borrow EH Carr's analogy of the historian as angler, there are plenty of fish to try and catch. Ultimately the authors I choose to publish are offering something I would want to read.

There is also in this selection of contributors a wilful arbitrariness rather than a subservience to a prescribed theme. I deliberately make *AA Files* free of any defining thematic partly as a way to set it apart from other architectural publications but also because – as much as it is sold as a journal's outward reflection of some known but previously uncategorised condition – the architectural theme seems to be an act of editorial narcissism, always projecting inwards (the easiest way to gain editorial recognition). I prefer the juxtapositions you get when you place ostensibly mismatching texts next to one another. In this I am guided by the clever paradox offered by Peter Eisenman's *Oppositions* – the journal's very name was oppositional and contradictory, but the nifty outlined P in Massimo Vignelli's graphic masthead also signalled an indifference (0 Positions), an acceptance of the notion of a certain intrinsic editorial neutrality. More than precedent, though, the idea of publishing a journal that simply finds itself informed by whatever happens to be passing seems more in keeping with the culture of the AA School. The AA that I like resides in its eclecticism. In the early issues of *AA Files* you see this in the co-existence of historians like Vidler, Middleton, Yates and Landau with designers like Cook, Coates and Tschumi. Indeed, the prevalence and importance attached to architectural history in this period – generally regarded as the high-watermark of the AA's design culture – is initially shocking but ultimately reassuring. And through this historicism, the first ten years of *AA Files* play themselves out less against the backdrop of those amazing first paintings by Zaha Hadid than they do through the brilliance of numerous essays by Robin Evans.

In the absence of a writerly voice as refined as Evans, the ability to generate and maintain a standard of writing is a constant editorial preoccupation. I like the essays in *AA Files* to be scholarly and rigorous but not overly academic (or at least not always predicated on academic propriety and weighed down by endless footnotes), and I like the structure of all pieces of writing to be linear not circular, so that the ends of essays offer ideas and subjects far removed from those introduced at their beginnings. Sometimes, achieving this effect means doing a bit of a Gordon Lish on the texts submitted to me (to really over-romanticise and escalate the importance of the editor), but at other times a more engaging and authentic voice can be achieved by relying on the spoken rather than the written word. People are generally more articulate when they talk than when they write. Boyarsky recognised this from the outset by offering the model of the transcribed lecture as an *AA Files* standard (a commitment to the idea of the academic as raconteur that continues at the AA today with a figure like Mark Cousins). Almost emblematically, you can see this in the first line from the first essay in the first ever issue: 'You probably know Sidney Smith's definition of paradise: "eating *pâté de foie gras* to the sound of trumpets". I think my definition of hell would be lecturing to the sound of bagpipes.' This is how the historian J Mordaunt Crook began his lecture, and subsequent essay, on London's clubland. Despite the fact that Crook associated lecturing with some kind of underworld perdition, this opening suggests that he lectured like an angel. More recently I have tried to resurrect this tradition by commissioning at least one conversation in every issue. I hope that this doesn't become formulaic (rather like the repeating model of Hans Ulrich Obrist's conversations with artists) but stays interesting and engaging (like the conversations with writers commissioned by the *Paris Review*).

As appealing as the paradigms offered by literature continue to be, more recent architectural writing seems to have thrown off its theoretical pretensions and embraced a return to narrative, recasting the architect as storyteller. Superficially this appears to represent everything that an editor would want – a renewed emphasis on the writerliness of the written word and the absorption of a set of literary allusions beyond architecture's typically small reference library. But as architects now increasingly revel in their own lyricism, what you get instead is all of the inviolability of literature, all of its self-importance, and none of its enjoyment. Even David Greene or Michael Webb, when reinventing the architectural project description in a prototypically narrative way, knew that their stuff wasn't to be taken entirely seriously. Now, however, there is no such mischief. There will come a point very soon when someone will launch a journal of literary writings by architects, and then there will be a time 20 years later when people will reread that journal and cringe.

Rather than any florid use of language, the thing that helps me convey the vernacular (in all senses of the word) of *AA Files* is its format and design. The physical quality of the journal is tremendously important. Acting out a well-rehearsed cliché of contemporary editorship, the first thing I did when I took over at *AA Files* was commission a redesign. The idea was not to create something so *à la mode* that it would have to be redesigned five years later, but to pare the journal down to the basics of its type, images and colours. I am very pleased with the result, not only because it allows me as editor to separate words from images by indulging in both, but because in generating its own nuances the graphics somehow mimic the AA – in particular, that strange and appealing confluence you get at the school of a residual Englishness overlaid with a polyglot internationalism.

In the end, though, as fond as I am of typefaces and essays, of the value of the journal and the liveliness of its authors, can't we challenge the editor a little more, or at least question their existence? Publishing houses within academic institutions always used to be somewhat peripheral enterprises – the university press on the edge of the campus. Over the last few years, however, academia's control over publishing has expanded to the point now where the self-generated book or magazine is not the culmination of any body of research but the beginning. Courses, curricula and programmes in schools of architecture seem to privilege the mediated, published text as never before. The consequence of this is that everyone seems to be editors. Made interchangeable with that other contemporary assignation, 'curator', editors of journals no longer have to deal only with their publishers and audience. Now academic directors want to edit, designers want to offer editorial consultation, writers want to be involved in the graphic conceit and your readership – in my case the entire student body of the AA – now seem so much more familiar with the lexicon of editing, graphic design and magazine production than they are with architecture. Ask students about the Tugendhat House and they will shrug their shoulders, but ask them about *S,M,L,XL* and they will give you a whole lecture on Bruce Mau. If you ask them to actually produce a magazine of their own you will have the whole thing – written, designed, printed – in front of you in no time at all. And so in the brief moment before I am usurped, and despite all my denials and a certain disdain, my last will and testament to architectural editorship is that all editors operate under their own 20 questions, their own guiding principles, regardless of how they are couched. For me, this is as close a diagram for any artistic, written or editorial endeavour as I could wish for:

Chapter One. He adored New York City. He idolised it all out of proportion'… er, no, make that, 'He romanticised it all out of proportion'. Yes. 'To him, no matter what the season, this was still a town that existed in black and white and pulsated to the great tunes of George Gershwin' … er, no, let me start this again. 'Chapter One. He was too romantic about Manhattan, as he was about everything else. He thrived on the hustle and bustle of the crowds and the traffic. To him, New York meant beautiful women and street-smart guys who seemed to know all the angles'… ah, corny, too corny for a man of my taste. Let me try and make it more profound. 'Chapter One. He adored New York City. To him, it was a metaphor for the decay of contemporary culture. The same lack of individual integrity that caused so many people to take the easy way out was rapidly turning the town of his dreams …', no, it's going be too preachy. Let's face it, I want to sell some books here. 'Chapter One. He adored New York City, although to him it was a metaphor for the decay of contemporary culture. How hard it was to exist in a society desensitised by drugs, loud music, television, crime, garbage …', too angry. I don't want to be angry. 'Chapter One. He was as tough and romantic as the city he loved. Behind his black-rimmed glasses was the coiled sexual power of a jungle cat.' I love this. 'New York was his town, and it always would be.'

137

HARVARD DESIGN MAGAZINE

Harvard University
Graduate School of Design
Architecture
Landscape architecture
Urban planning and design
Spring/Summer 2010

32

$23 US/28.95 CDN

DESIGN PRACTICES NOW VOL. I

HARVARD DESIGN MAGAZINE

William S Saunders

1. Acts of judgement ('criticality') are inevitable in all aspects of editing – selecting topics, questions to address, subject matter, writers, writing approach, photography, graphics, order of presentation, etc. All these must be non-arbitrary choices, choices based on some sense of values: what matters, what doesn't, what needs attention, what is trivial, what kind of content is appropriate for anticipated readers, etc. Even in the presentation of 'facts', there is no neutrality, since not only deciding what facts to present, but also what deserves to be called a 'fact', involves judgement.

2. Deciding what issues and questions need thoughtful consideration is the biggest responsibility for any editor. To do this, editors not only have to have sensitive antennae to pick up signals from all available sources (publications, other people, the physical environments they encounter…), they should also spend most of their 'free' time actively and extensively trying to bring in these signals. Perhaps unfortunately, that means almost constantly reading scores of periodicals and books in the fields of architecture, landscape architecture, urban design, urban planning and related fields just to 'keep up'. But 'keeping up' also means more general reading of things like the *New York Times* and the *New York Review of Books*. The misfortune is that subjects and thinking

from beyond the design disciplines – art, philosophy, history, sociology, literature, science, etc – are not given enough attention. And reading for mindless relaxation never seems possible.

3. Offering opinions is easy; anyone can do it. Offering research, analysis, understanding, fresh and important information and supported judgement is hard. The editor has to seek out writers who have done or will do this hard work, taking the time it needs for a responsible and careful job. Why read anything unless you expect to learn more than opinion?

4. I can't 'determine' if the editorial statement (the brief for contributors) is 'valid', only that it seems to hold up to scrutiny and earns positive responses from respected/ respectable others who know the subject matter well.

5. Always. A set of questions that have ready and certain answers would not be interesting or important. I plan feature topics on the basis of their needing but not yet having resolution. Now, for instance, I am working on an issue whose goal is to determine ways in which architecture can pursue beauty and sustainability simul- taneously, with complete integration. This is only inter- esting if architects tend to pursue primarily beauty OR sustainability, with one normally weakening the other.

6. I expect readers to have opinions on ALL the issues I raise but to realise that their opinions always need to be better informed and thought through.

7. Ideally, a thematic issue would instigate intense debate, discussion and self-questioning. But some topics, however important, may generate harmonious consensus, even if

that consensus is relatively new. Readers may agree (and have always thought) that there are universal problems with learning about buildings only through photographs, yet it may be important to spell out those problems in detail and bring them more fully into consciousness. On the other hand, whether skyscrapers are or can be a sustainable green building type is by no means clear and settled, yet this is a more important issue than the limitations of architectural photography.

8. Not necessarily. All the essays in a non-thematic issue could be polemical. I do hope that everything in *Harvard Design Magazine* has at least some polemical undercurrent – otherwise, who should care?

9. 'Frivolousness'? That sounds like irresponsibly not taking the subject matter seriously. But humour and satire – most definitely. In *HDM*, Michael Sorkin mocked contemporary urban design with devastating wit. His sword struck more deeply than ponderous straightness could have.

10. The best essays challenge, destroy or discombobulate the orthodoxies of received opinion.

11. A publication that is merely a basket into which several people are free to throw whatever they like is more likely to be flat and aimless – boring. And editing by committee, while it is good to ensure diversity of view-points, is unwieldy and often chaotic. The publication needs to have an edge, and this comes from one person's convictions and/or leadership. Ideally, however, that one person will seek and use the input of many people, some of whom disagree with him or her.

12. The only issue here, I think, is images – can they be large enough? Can there be as many as are needed? Can all that should be in colour be in colour? A small black and white journal or magazine will have trouble conveying the realities of architecture.

13. Your question is unclear. *HDM* seeks to be simultaneously scholarly and critical – it is a publication of well-supported ideas. It is not interested in facts for facts' sake. Most of its items are not 'peer reviewed', and this allows it to be more agile and less conventional. Yes, universities should support pure scholarship that is peer reviewed: the expansion of real knowledge for its own sake is a necessary goal.

14. Impossible to generalise. Academia is still, for the most part, full of Gradgrinds and Casaubons who are terrified of going outside a zone of lifeless 'neutrality' and 'fact'-collecting into grounded assertions about important truths. If a teacher has personal beliefs and a curator is a mere collector, we need more teachers.

15. Insofar as any course establishes as its goal the obtaining of new understanding and knowledge (through research and/or design), it will potentially produce material worthy of publication. Most courses don't do this; rather they share established knowledge and ideas. At Harvard an effort is being made to make more courses voyages of discovery. Some courses could have, from the start, an explicit goal of producing material appropriate to *HDM* – this would be a productive spur to hard cutting-edge classroom work.

16. Not really. The proof is in the pudding. I would be delighted to publish any brilliant and important essay without knowing anything about the author's biography.

17. In every way possible: by exploring and evaluating recent works of architecture; by critiquing the structures, rules, conventions and mores of architecture practice; by critically analysing limited and limiting conventions of thought, etc.

18. I don't defend them. I do the best I can to determine what matters, then send forth the little boat...

19. Design as criticism and research deserves more attention than *HDM* has given it.

20. n/a

THE FUNCTION OF ORNAMENT

EDITED BY FARSHID MOUSSAVI AND MICHAEL KUBO

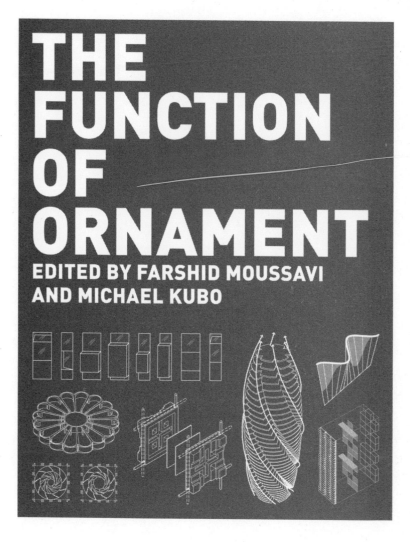

ACTAR

Michael Kubo

The history of architecture is closely related to the history of books produced by architects. Just as buildings produce discourses in and of themselves, so the strategic discourse of the book has often been used by architects to excavate a conceptual space in which (their) buildings can be both produced and understood. Many of the most prominent architects of the past century have also been prolific publishers and editors; the production of architecture has been inseparable from the production of its related discourse – through magazines, journals, treatises, manifestoes, monographs, pamphlets, transcripts, films, interviews – as parallel strands of work that are assumed to support each other, but which in reality often reveal a provocative (and in some cases deliberate) misalignment. Publishing is an operative weapon in the architect's arsenal, deployed for its unique capacity to frame the practice of the architect and to perform as a critical form of architecture itself. Publications can be understood as a strategic mode of architectural practice, parallel to (and frequently more agile than) forms of production more typically understood as architectural.

Beyond direct examples of editorial and publishing practice by architects, the two fields are deeply imbricated and mutually dependent. Editors, curators and publishers cannot be regarded as external to architectural practice; they are crucial actors in the production of architectural agendas, just as engineers, contractors and fabricators are crucial actors in the production of buildings. If the editorial process shares certain similarities to the processes of architectural production, it is also fundamentally different from the conventional idea of authorship. The editorial process is essentially one of curation, based on the accumulation of a density of material within a project – not just of different forms of content but also sources, references, ideas, relationships, agendas – that is then mediated and structured through strategic choices in selection, structure, weight, rhythm, pacing and language (both visual and textual). In this sense editing should be regarded less as a discipline separate from architecture than as a methodology that can be applied equally to the production of books and buildings. This method must be judged differently from the typical idea of the author-architect as the generator of 'original' work; instead, the practice of the editor involves the mediation of a density of forces and intentions that condense within the physical space of a project, whether that space manifests itself in published or architectural production.

* * *

The following pages show examples of editorial practice from *The Function of Ornament*, co-edited with Farshid Moussavi and published by Actar Editorial. The book grew out of a Harvard GSD seminar in Spring 2006 that was explicitly intended to produce graphical research on ornament in book form. The agenda to treat the project as a process of book production provided immediate constraints to the research, subjecting the work to both editorial and architectural criteria from the outset. All seminar materials were presented exclusively in page layouts (mockups were produced weekly), so that the graphic research was constantly forced to address issues of format, layout, the number and relationships of drawings on each page, sequence and rhythm, and the role of text, in addition to the architectural concerns of the course.

The seminar was organised from the beginning as a graphic comparison of selected examples of twentieth-century ornament. Students began with an initial list of 150 possible cases; over the course of the semester these were condensed or replaced (with additional examples added along the way) to reach a final list of 42 prototypical cases; these were eventually limited to the twentieth century and to built projects only as further constraints to the research. Both the graphic methods that were developed to compare cases and the information that was produced were crucial in deciding which cases were ultimately included, how to classify them, and what conclusions could be drawn from their comparison.

The editorial agenda of the book was positioned from the beginning between two existing types of publication: technical publications that describe the details behind building skin systems but are inadequate to show the effects they generate; and glossy magazines or coffee-table books that are devoted to showing these effects without describing how or why they are produced. The 'section-perspective' (a true section cut with building surfaces seen in one-point perspective) that became the critical technique to bridge these two types of information emerged out of a series of drawing types that were tested through an evolving set of production methods, starting with conventional forms of 2D drawing and ultimately requiring a complex composite of 3D digital modelling with rendering and line drawing techniques. (The development of these techniques to produce the drawings digitally was an interesting by-product of the research, since the use of the sectional or cutaway perspective as a composite drawing type was not uncommon before the advent of the computer, most famously by Paul Rudolph.)

The combination of a practitioner and an editor as instructors meant that the agendas guiding the project were at once directed toward the two practices of architecture and publishing. While the references for the book's arguments about ornament are outlined in the introductory text, the editorial project involved a parallel set of precedents for drawing techniques and the graphic manual as a form, including Roger Sherwood's *Modern Housing Prototypes*, Edwin Ford's *The Details of Modern Architecture*, and Atelier Bow-Wow's *Made In Tokyo*. These and other examples were studied for their use of drawing techniques and their successes or failures as specific graphic languages, particularly in their use of graphic consistency as a structuring device across a set of comparative information.

The final relation between content and form in *The Function of Ornament* reflects a set of questions about the reception, duration and legibility of the editorial agendas contained in the project: Can a theoretical argument be embedded in the form of a manual? Could the final form of the book be situated equally within the category of current practice-oriented guides and the historical lineage of treatises on function and ornament? What kinds of architectural knowledge can be produced through graphical analysis? Can the development of drawing techniques constitute a form of architectural research?

The result is an integrated product that combines drawing, text, layout, page sequence and classification into an editorial whole. The book cannot be understood conventionally as a set of textual arguments 'illustrated' by graphics, nor could it have been produced through a conventional relationship between author, editor and publisher. Editorial and architectural concerns are bound together in the form of the book; the graphic structure and organisation of the book themselves constitute the theoretical content of the research. This integration is reflected in the following pages, showing comments (at once architectural and editorial) made on the various mockups produced during the course of the project.

CONTENTS

RE-ORDER OF CHAPTERS:
INTRINSIC → EXTRINSIC
Form, Construction, Screen,
Light, Pattern, Signification

The organisation of cases and chapters changed continuously throughout the project. Cases were tested at certain points on a spectrum between ornament and décor, at other times categorised in terms of the types of effects produced (effects based on light, signification, pattern, etc). Eventually cases were ordered along a gradient according to the material required to produce the ornamental effect, from the most 'intrinsic' (those that rely on a deep relation to the interior of the building) to the most 'extrinsic' (those with the thinnest relation to the interior, as in blank types, where the interior content is largely irrelevant to the effect).

The chapters were finally condensed to four – Form, Structure, Screen, Surface – and ordered along this gradient from deepest to thinnest (according to the degree of relation between the building interior and the effect, different from the literal depth of the envelope.)

ment is achieved through the discretization of building elements into a mechanical core and basic dwelling unit, or capsule, as the generative onent of the façade. The aggregation of individual capsules reveals the construction methodologies: prefabrication, transportation, assemblage, and an obsolescence.

1 This still looks like an axo rather than effect dwg.

2 Simplify to circle them.

As different formats for the 'effect spread' were tested, it was decided that all affect images would run full-bleed (ie, extend to the limits of the double page), never showing the edges of the building, in order to emphasise the ornamental pattern alone. The viewpoint for each effect drawing varies from elevation to perspective or axonometric depending on the qualities to be shown in the specific case.

1. This still looks like an axo[nometric] rather than an effect dwg.

2. Simplify to circle only.

The effect drawing is not an attempt to show the literal appearance of the building, but an abstract graphic that shows only those visual elements that are necessary to produce the ornamental effect. In each case, any visual details that do not contribute to the effect are removed. In this case (Kurokawa's Capsule Hotel), this included the radial infill of the circular windows and the seams between panels of the prefabricated apartment units.

Final version

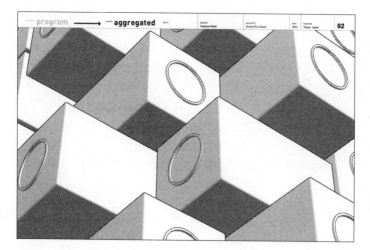

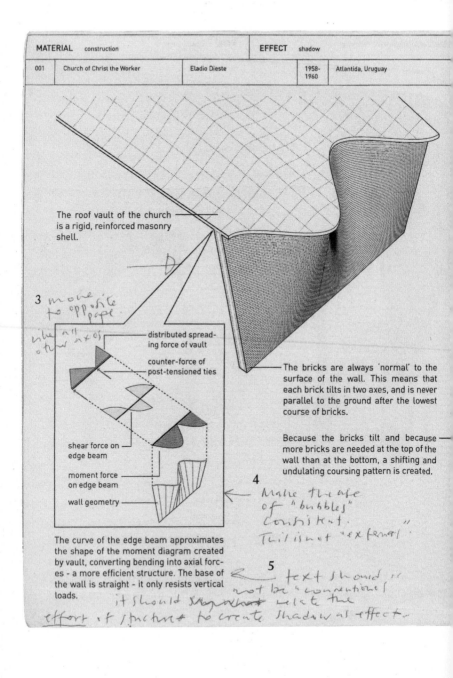

The roof vault of the church is a rigid, reinforced masonry shell.

3 *move to opposite page*

like all other axes

distributed spread-ing force of vault

counter-force of post-tensioned ties

shear force on edge beam

moment force on edge beam

wall geometry

The bricks are always 'normal' to the surface of the wall. This means that each brick tilts in two axes, and is never parallel to the ground after the lowest course of bricks.

Because the bricks tilt and because more bricks are needed at the top of the wall than at the bottom, a shifting and undulating coursing pattern is created.

4 *Make the one of "bubbles" consistent. This is not "external".*

The curve of the edge beam approximates the shape of the moment diagram created by vault, converting bending into axial forces - a more efficient structure. The base of the wall is straight - it only resists vertical loads.

5 *text should not be "conventional". it should say what like the effort of structure to create shadow as effect.*

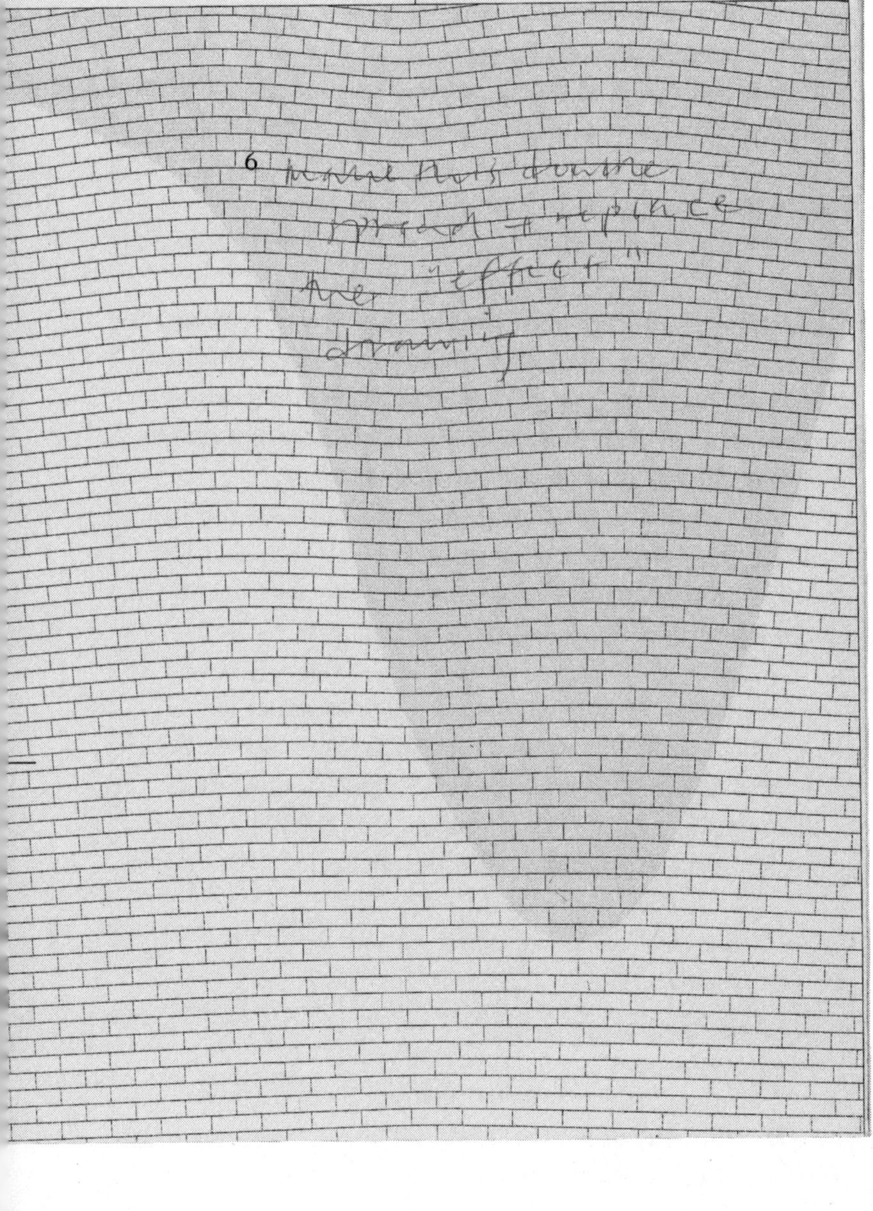
6

3. Move to opposite page like all other
axo[nometric]s.

As the drawings developed, the graphic system became more
consistent across cases: each 'material' double spread is always
based on a synthetic drawing on the right page (eventually a
section-perspective, but here a cutaway axonometric), with
relevant details and additional information on the left page.

4. Make the use of 'bubbles' consistent.
This is not 'exterior'.

A system of graphic 'bubbles' was initially tested to show the
extrinsic factors (programmatic, cultural or physical forces)
that condition the intrinsic formal decisions that generate
the ornament in each case. This information was eventually
absorbed into the captions to the main drawings.

5. Text should not be 'conventional' it should
relate the effort of structure to create shadow as effect.

Any architectural information that was inessential to
the production of the ornamental effect was removed. The
structural diagram became the key graphic to show the
relation between the structural forces of the double-curved
roof vaults and the undulation of the enclosing walls beneath.

6. Make this double spread + replace the
'effect' drawing.

This was a first example of what would eventually become the
format for the effect spreads: an abstract pattern (running to
the edges of the double page) that graphically reproduces the
effect produced in each case.

Final versions

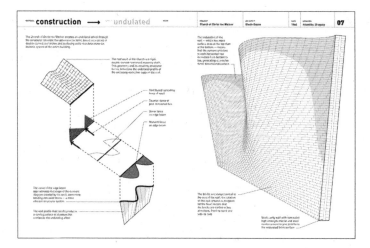

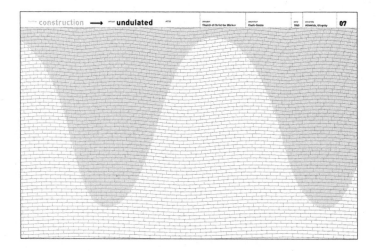

construction → undulated   Church of Christ the Worker   Eladio Dieste   1960   Atlántida, Uruguay   07

161

material		effect
light	⟶	**banding**

In the Johnson Wax Laboratory Tower double-height bands of horizontal glass tubes replace the conventional strip windows of the office tower, acting as a light filter between interior and exterior. Combined with an alternating pattern of floors and mezzanine levels in section and the rounded corners of its profile, the effect is an expression of the tower as a banded column whose interior contents are registered as blurred presences on the exterior.

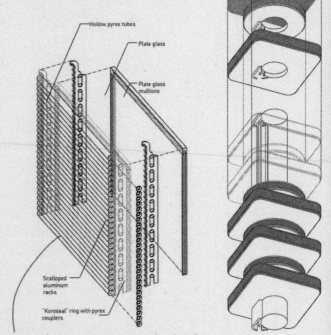

Hollow pyrex tubes

Plate glass

Plate glass mullions

Scalloped aluminum racks

"Koroseal" ring with pyrex couplers

Right now it is "photo", not a pattern.

project	architect	date	location	
Johnson Wax Laboratory Tower	Frank Lloyd Wright	1950	Racine, US	33

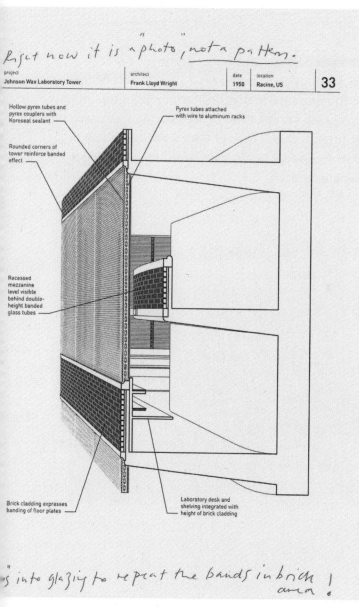

Hollow pyrex tubes and pyrex couplers with Koroseal sealant

Pyrex tubes attached with wire to aluminum racks

Rounded corners of tower reinforce banded effect

Recessed mezzanine level visible behind double-height banded glass tubes

Brick cladding expresses banding of floor plates

Laboratory desk and shelving integrated with height of brick cladding

"s into glazing to repeat the bands in brick! area.

7. I think effect drawing should be just an elevation. This precedes lots of banded projects
of Sejima + others + it is more powerful in elevation. Right now it is a 'photo', not a pattern.

The effect spreads are not intended to represent a literal
'image' of each building; rather, they are abstract drawings
that attempt to reproduce in distilled form, within the graphic space of the book, the qualities of the effect in each case.
As a graphic project, this is in may ways a more difficult task
than that of conventional renderings, based on achieving a
photorealistic appearance.

Draft version

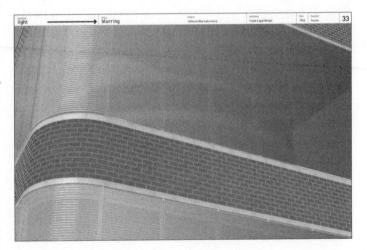

Final version

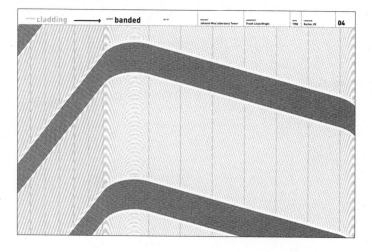

8. Could we talk about these as micro-bands? As a self-similarity of the larger band[ed] order? Otherwise this detail is redundant. It is interesting that [Wright] builds 'coursings' in the glazing to repeat the bands in [the] brick area!

Final version

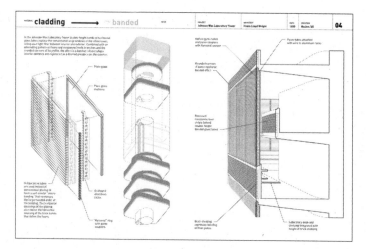

9 The Ehrs..... Library explores seriality as an effect.

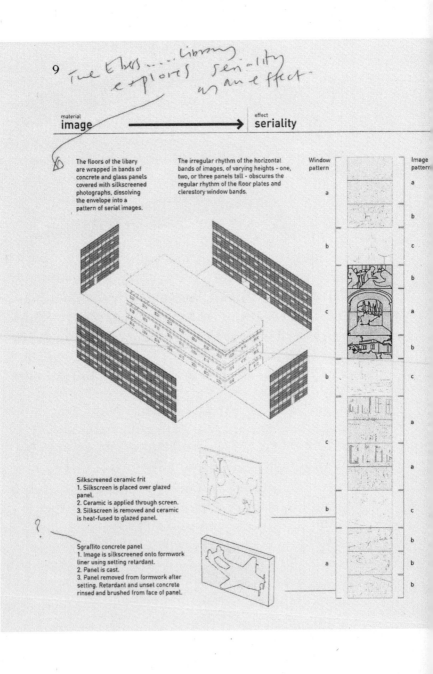

material
image ———————————————→ effect
seriality

The floors of the libary are wrapped in bands of concrete and glass panels covered with silkscreened photographs, dissolving the envelope into a pattern of serial images.

The irregular rhythm of the horizontal bands of images, of varying heights - one, two, or three panels tall - obscures the regular rhythm of the floor plates and clerestory window bands.

Window pattern

a

b

c

b

c

Image pattern

a

b

c

b

a

b

c

a

a

c

b

b

b

Silkscreened ceramic frit
1. Silkscreen is placed over glazed panel.
2. Ceramic is applied through screen.
3. Silkscreen is removed and ceramic is heat-fused to glazed panel.

?

Sgraffito concrete panel
1. Image is silkscreened onto formwork liner using setting retardant.
2. Panel is cast.
3. Panel removed from formwork after setting. Retardant and unset concrete rinsed and brushed from face of panel.

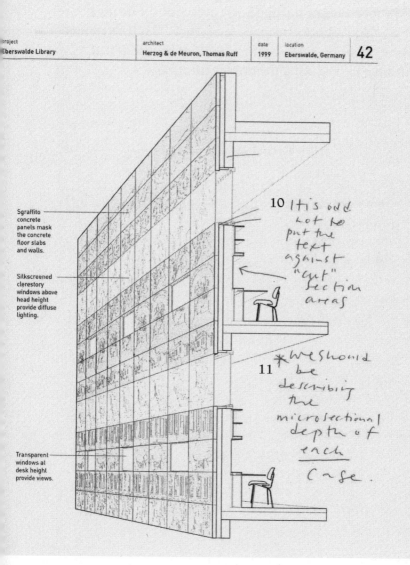

Sgraffito concrete panels mask the concrete floor slabs and walls.

Silkscreened clerestory windows above head height provide diffuse lighting.

Transparent windows at desk height provide views.

10 It is odd not to put the text against "cut" section areas

11 *We should be describing the microsectional depth of each case.

9. The Ebers[walde] Library explores seriality as an effect.

Each case eventually acquired a short introductory paragraph (consistent graphically with the captions to drawings, but always appearing in the upper left corner of the material spread) that describes the intended affect. All other captions were edited to focus on specific details or decisions that contribute to producing the overall affect.

Final version

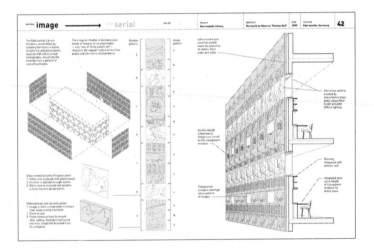

10. It is odd not to put the text against 'cut' section areas

11. * We should be describing the micro-sectional depth of each case.

The section-perspective (a composite of a true section cut with elevation seen in perspective behind) became the key document to reveal the relation between the construction of the envelope (section) and the affect it produces (perspective). These drawings are consistent for all cases in orientation and composition, versus the more variable information on the left page of each material spread. Captions for section-perspectives are focused on the 'micro-depth' of the section cut, where the relation between construction and affect is most apparent.

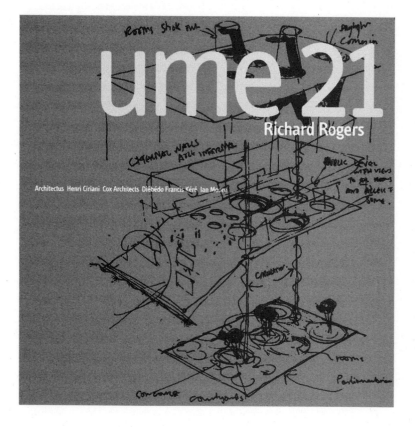

ume 21

Richard Rogers

Architectus Henri Ciriani Cox Architects Diébédo Francis Kéré Ian Moore

UME

Haig Beck & Jackie Cooper

To edit: vt 1a: to prepare an edition of... b: to
assemble by cutting and rearranging c: to alter,
adapt, or refine esp. to bring about conformity
to a standard or to suit a particular purpose
2: to direct the publication of... 3: delete...
Webster's New Collegiate Dictionary

We edit drawings, specifically the working drawings
architects make to build their designs. *UME* may be the only
magazine to do this.

We do edit texts, but it is not our primary task as the
editors and publishers of *UME*. We edit architects' statements
about their work to make them intelligible and succinct.
Occasionally we commission texts, and these we edit for style
and consistency and to eliminate jargon.

We also write, mostly in the form of caption texts of
about 150 words containing our observations on the buildings
we publish. Our captions are not descriptive, but about
architectural ideas and theory which we try to make relevant
to practising architects.

Architects' working drawings contain many layers of
technical information, a lot of it contractual or dealing with
code compliance. Using Photoshop, we edit out this information (delete) and reinforce the line work (adapt, refine) to
clarify and distinguish between levels of information. Like all
editing, it is a painstaking process, and at times we have spent
weeks digitally manipulating a single drawing, pixel by pixel.
True to the best editorial principles of working with an

author, we don't standardise the drawings but rather enhance and elucidate the architect's drawn *voice*. We do this with subtlety: architects generally remain unaware of the extent to which we have worked on their drawings.

We make architectural magazines that we expect only practising architects will read. It is gratifying when academics read them and comment favourably, but essentially we see our readership as architects (and students) who aspire to make buildings.

Reading Drawings

Why do architects read architectural magazines? Not to put too fine a point on it: in order to find ideas for their own designs. That is not to say that copying is bad. The act of copying is an act of transformation, as is all design. However, there is always risk associated with copying. At best, uncritical copying results in stylistic, decorative scenography, and at worst it produces architectural malapropisms.

So to confront the problem of superficial copying, we set about manipulating the reader. We tend only to publish working drawings in *UME*. These are not the standardised drawings normally seen in magazines, stripped clean for publication, but coded diagrams encrypted with information about the very stuff of a building – materials and their detailing. These are drawings that architects are trained to read; they require deciphering. In that process of deciphering, something happens. The reader begins to construct the building mentally. That process requires that readers deconstruct the drawings first in order to construct the design in their heads.

One of the ways we force this process is by withholding coloured images. Photographs of the completed building are reproduced in black and white. This is a way of abstracting the image of the building and further engaging the reader's critical imagination. We publish only two or three photographs of a building. A reader is left to infer from clues in the encrypted drawings and the few photographs what the building is like. Reading the drawings is not a passive act of soaking up glossy images.

Consequently our readership is confined, and *UME*'s print-run tiny by commercial standards. (However, as we discovered lately, *UME*'s readership has exploded since we made the magazine available online with free downloads.)

Developing a Position

For us, architectural publishing is self-indulgence (as *UME*'s small print-run attests). We do it because we like to think about architecture; and having gone to the trouble, publishing is irresistible.

We are our ideal reader, and that conceit sets us apart from most other editors who, realistically, must consider seriously the nature and interests of their readerships and satisfy also the demands of advertisers and marketing departments. (Long ago we realised that advertising is the tail that wags the editorial dog and decided not to be co-opted, preferring complete editorial independence.) We don't see how *UME* in its present incarnation could exist under the direction of other editors, not through arrogance, but because we have created a publication in our own image, as it were, that reflects specifically the architectural interests and position of its editors; and those interests are becoming more esoteric as we age (currently we are reconsidering classicism, not a likely proposition for increasing sales). Moreover, since we launched *UME* in 1996, we have encountered no other magazine emulating our fascination with working drawings, wisely it would seem, since editing drawings is an endlessly meticulous task for apparently only slight gain, an impractical waste of time for any magazine with commercial underpinnings. Being our own essential reader, we express our editorial voice most clearly in terms of the material we choose to publish – and equally in terms of what we choose not to publish. It is true that we're aware that certain issues of *UME* have sold more quickly than others, and this makes any editor take stock. We are not perverse: we try our best to make all our editions beautiful, interesting, useful. However, we know of no sure formula to guarantee the popularity of an edition. We simply stick with what interests or intrigues us. In this way, we have sustained over the years a small, constant readership of like souls who appreciate *UME*'s qualities; and before that, readers joined us readily on a journey of discovery with *AD* and *International Architect*. We don't believe that people edit architectural magazines as the means to own a Porsche or BMW. We suspect that most editors, like us, are impelled by another order of motive. In our case it's pedagogy. In the early days, we were learning through editing; now we teach through editing.

When Haig first began editing *Architectural Design* in 1976 (for quite a time he had no staff, and ever since we've worked as a unit), it was from the advantageous position of knowing that we knew nothing really about architecture. Following in the footsteps of the great technical editors of *AD* – Theo Crosby, Ken Frampton, Robin Middleton, Peter Murray – Haig carried on the *AD* tradition of commissioning thematic issues, inviting the best minds to be guest editors and contributors. Coinciding with a major exhibition at the Hayward Gallery, Dalibor Vesely directed an issue on Surrealism – at the time not an obvious architectural subject (*AD* 2–3/78). Antoine Grumbach guest-edited the bi-lingual 'France, les laboratoires de l'architecture' (*AD* 8–9/78); the French emphasis on theory was revelatory to Anglo empiricists. When 'London 1900' was published (which included a map guide, another *AD* tradition), it was quite bizarre to present Edwardian architecture to a sophisticated architectural readership (*AD* 5–6/78). But we were following our instincts and interests, always eclectic. *AD* in those years covered the gamut from garbage housing to high-tech. Another historicist issue resulted when the Architectural Association's General Studies supremo, Robin Middleton, organised an exhibition and conference on the Beaux-Arts at the school and guest-edited an edition of *AD* (11–12/78). 'Roma Interrotta', guest-edited by Michael Graves, featured projects based on Nolli's 1748 plan of Rome (another exhibition at the AA), and included Caroline Constant's sixteenth-century Mannerist Rome map guide (*AD* 3–4/79). Joseph Rykwert guest-edited 'Leonis Baptiste Alberti' (*AD* 5–6/79), publishing the only extant drawing by Alberti, newly discovered by Howard Burns; Joseph asked Cecil Grayson, Hubert Damisch, Françoise Choay and Manfredo Tafuri to contribute essays.

As a young editor, the experience of putting together these issues of *AD* was akin to participating in a series of stimulating, high-powered tutorials. It was a hell of an education; and a lot of the readers thought so too. We doubled *AD*'s circulation.

In addition to what we learned from the subject matter of these issues, we discovered progressively that editing teaches you how to think: to structure ideas. Learning the thinking skills doesn't come overnight: it takes years – not to mention also developing a position from which to edit.

Our choice of the thematic topics was diverse. We were interested in everything; and it became a question of which ideas could be supported through the editorial process and the widening circle of contacts we made editing *AD*, and those were the topics we ran with. Commissioning as an editor remains a very opportunistic exercise. The trick is to see the connections.

Our work editing *AD* (and later, *International Architect*) was made possible by Alvin Boyarsky's patronage and our access to the Architectural Association. Haig was (nominally) still a student at the AA, and Jackie worked in the Communications Unit with Dennis Crompton throughout the 1970s, videoing the major lectures and putting together exhibitions and catalogues. It was during this period that Alvin as Chairman turned the AA School into the most exciting centre of architecture in the world. The students, year masters and visitors included David Chipperfield, Zaha Hadid, Rem Koolhaas, Will Alsop, Bernard Tschumi, Piers Gough, Roy Landau, Robin Evans, Elia Zenghelis, Peter Cook, Cedric Price, Fred Scott, the Smithsons, Michael Graves, James Stirling, Bob Maxwell, Tony Vidler, Richard Rogers... all of whom we published. Being at the AA nearly every day, it was natural that many *AD* editions should arise out of conversations and events there. Fuelled by ideological and theoretical extremes, the AA hothouse nurtured a thousand flowers, and this plurality would lay the ground for our catholic editorial bent.

It was still a time of extraordinary editorial independence (circulation was rising, but ultimately *AD*'s publisher would meddle intolerably). Haig asked Charles Jencks to write 'Isozaki and Radical Eclecticism' for an issue on Arata Isozaki (*AD* 1/77)'. He then commissioned Charles to develop his theory and write the first *AD* book, working title, 'Radical Eclecticism' – what resulted a few months later was *The Language of Post-Modern Architecture*. We published Léon Krier on type and *quartiers*, the first time he appeared in English (*AD* 3/77). Rem Koolhaas was unknown when a whole issue was devoted to OMA (*AD* 5/77). Bruce Goff, architectural lovechild of Frank Lloyd Wright, lectured at the AA, and we were inspired to devote an issue to his work (*AD* 10/78). Europeans at the time could not make sense of Goff: the camp iconoclasm made reference neither to modernism nor to an ideological social framework; yet he was among the most innovative form-givers of the twentieth century, and even more significant perhaps were his phenomenological, experiential explorations of architecture, something that we still don't have a ready vocabulary for or the conceptual means to discuss. In the issue we reproduced 16 pages of raw working drawing blueprints (in 1978 you would never see such drawings in a magazine), sparking an editorial fascination with working drawings that has powered all our work since.

Much of the material we featured in *AD* was then at the edges of the architectural mainstream. For instance, 'Handbuilt Hornby Island' – an issue on buildings at the interface between architecture and craft constructed from flotsam and jetsam by owner-builders on an island off the west coast of Canada (*AD* 7/78) – was just what architecture magazines did not feature. Previous *AD* editors had drawn on other disciplines to expand the discourse: social theory and philosophy (Robin Middleton), new technology futures (Peter Murray), alternative technology and sustainability (Martin Spring). With our catholic editorial choices, we were pushing the boundaries of what was admissible in architectural discourse, examining architectural ideas in light of classicism, history, art and a contemporary counter-culture ethos, always from the perspective of design.

We had sensed that a major paradigm shift was occurring, away from the model of the architect as social engineer to one of culturally critical practitioner. This shift was given impetus by the Europeans – the French, Italians and Spaniards. The shift was apparent from the outset of editing *AD*. 'Volte Face', the first issue that Haig and Martin Spring edited together (*AD* 3/76) included an editorial that set out their position: 'In every facet of architecture and the built environment there are signs of radical changes having taken place over the past decade. In aggregate, these changes amount to a volte face on a scale of the inception of the Modern Movement during the 1920s. However, the volte face of the 70s seems to have occurred in the opposite direction to the heroic approach of the 20s which attempted to wipe the slate clean with a brand new, rational and universal theory of architecture...The volte face in architecture...has certainly been no crisp about turn of a well-drilled squad of professionals. Rather, it resembles fall out at the end of a parade in which small groups wander off informally in diverse directions. It is all the more important, then, that those attempting to understand the new directions in architecture should try to delve into the root causes of the many disparate, sometimes contradictory, and often deceptive current trends.' Aware of an apparent pluralism, they set out to investigate whether there was an underlying conceptual and philosophical structure to this volte face.

In hindsight, we realise that these *AD*s reveal something of the zeitgeist/discourses of the time. Alternative technology, history and postmodernism were challenges to the apparently exhausted modernist canon. Only a few in those days, including Rem, saw the modernist light on the hill still burned.

Quest for Editorial Freedom

Our last edition of *AD* was to be the issue on Alberti guest-edited by Joseph Rykwert (*AD* 5–6/79). The publisher interfered over the choice of the cover image, one instance too many of editorial meddling. Haig resigned on the spot and the next day we began raising funds to start *International Architect*. This break was really about changing editorial direction. The decade-long freeze on building in Britain imposed by a weak economy (and the oil crisis in 1973) was beginning to thaw, and architects were building again.

Having spent an intense three years producing thematic issues, we wanted to spread our wings and publish contemporary design work – and buildings. But *AD*'s publisher did not want to upset the successful, lucrative thematic publishing formula we had developed.

In *International Architect, an international review of architectural projects, theory, practice and criticism* we published contemporary architecture. We wanted to make a magazine as beautiful as the buildings we were going to publish: *International Architect* was about design and had to express this design ethos. We chose a large, almost square format and called in Swiss typographer, Roland Schenk. Unlike *AD*'s rather smudgy printing, *International Architect* was sharp and clean: ideal for showing drawings on a large scale, often as full-page bleeds and double-page spreads. We lavished space on featured works, giving each a dozen pages or so. There was colour, a proper spine, quality paper stocks. It felt like driving a Citroën DS after a 2CV.

Our good friend, David Dunster, joined us as an Associate Editor in 1982, contributing academic rigour and a dash of irony to *International Architect*'s editorial voice.

International Architect issue 9 (1982), featuring Robert Venturi, James Gowan and Purini and Thermes, was an editorial milestone. It presents the working drawings of three houses built using three different technologies from three different cultural backgrounds, and explains the various cultural and technological impacts. This editorial work (fully expressed here for the first time) of selection and exegesis epitomises our approach of exploring the impacts of regional factors on modernism.

We published the next nine issues as *UIA International Architect* (the UIA raised sponsorship) and returned to editing thematics, now based on regionalism, and significantly on the nexus between modernism and regional practice (as presaged in Issue 9). The first issue of *UIA*

International Architect was 'L'Architecture Nouvelle. France after 68: Theory into Practice'. Other regional issues followed on Madrid, Australia, Southern Africa, Malaysia, Islamic Cairo and Israel.

Raising funding through the UIA was patchy. Mostly we needed to raise sponsorship ourselves. Peter Palumbo made it possible to publish issue 3, 'Mies van der Rohe: Mansion House Square and the Tower Type'. While as editors we were keen to investigate alternatives, we have always been fundamentally interested in modern architecture and at every opportunity have encouraged work on the great, unfinished modernist project.

In 1984, the RIBA asked us to edit its pre-conference papers. Typical of our editorial pragmatism and publishing opportunism, we realised that if we published these papers as an issue of *UIA International Architect*, we could also include the work that Roy Landau had been carrying out with his students at the AA Graduate School on the British contribution to the modernist project. This is probably the most important set of texts we have ever published (issue 5).

We ended the relationship with the UIA in 1985 after their lawyers based in Paris sent a peremptory letter demanding we relinquish the UIA's title, *International Architect*. The arrogance of this assumption of our title was too much. We'd had enough. It was time to close the magazine and return to Australia.

It would be nearly ten years before we started to publish again. The first *UME*s were hand-made, loose-leafed sheaves of (beautifully) photocopied architectural drawings, collected in a cedar box. Then in 1996 we resumed publishing in earnest, with a printed *UME* designed by Garry Emery.

We have produced 21 issues of *UME*. Publishing from Australia suggested an editorial change of emphasis. *UME*, international in scope, has an obvious bias towards the Antipodes. Initially we saw this as redressing eurocentric architectural publishing. But we got over that. The rapid development of a web-based global culture meant that it is no longer necessary to feel confined to a particular geographic zone. Another facet of this technological phenomenon is that it's not necessary to be based in a big city either; we edit *UME* from a subtropical island.

Buildings or Projects?

Thirty years on, we have a developed editorial position, although the selection of material in *UME* is as eclectic and opportunistic as our inclusions in *AD* and *International Architect*. We rarely publish projects. They are not tested in the same way as built designs that must answer the realities of place, economics and programme; nor are they tested by the degree of resolution required to bring a design into concrete reality. Our choice of buildings to publish in *UME* recognises the constructive rigour an architect needs to realise a design idea. And while our selections will often seem catholic, in reality there is a strong theoretical position that we promote, and it is this:

'The built invariably comes into existence out of the constantly evolving interplay of three converging vectors: the topos, the typos, and the tectonic. And while the tectonic does not necessarily favour any particular style, it does in conjunction with the site and type, serve to counter the present tendency for architecture to derive its legitimacy from some other discourses.' – Kenneth Frampton, *Studies in Tectonic Culture*, MIT Press, 1995.

We remain in Frampton's debt for elegantly codifying this position.

Our Editorial Position

We are not practising architects, so in that sense we don't have an architectural position. But we do see ourselves through the magazine as pedagogues with an architectural/editorial position.

We take the view that the substance of architecture – the topos, typos and tectonics – forms the foundation upon which the edifice of architectural theory, criticism and practice should be erected.

Topos deals with the local determinants associated with place, climate and topography.

Typology – the typos – is the architectural strategy for making building forms that are culturally connected to a place, its people and their programmes. This legacy of cultural connection is not constrained by historicism or nostalgia. Abstraction frees architects to transform existing typologies and create new forms and meanings within a cultural continuum.

The practice of tectonics raises to poetic expression the building materials and construction techniques that belong to a particular place and time.

Le Corbusier ended *Vers une architecture* with the proposition: 'architecture or revolution'. We don't see architecture, as Le Corbusier did, as the counter to social revolution. But we subscribe to the redemptive power of architecture, its capacity to dignify human life. We use the word *redemptive* not in any religious sense but to mean the saving or improving of something that has declined into a poor state. It is our belief that the redemptive power of architecture depends on practice critically grounded in the topos, typos and tectonics of a culture.

Theory vs Practice,
Architecture's Own Voice

Roy Landau, who headed the AA Graduate School for many years, observed: 'there are strong Anglo-Saxon attitudes upheld in the British architectural context, and perhaps most pervasive is the tendency towards empiricism. This long-standing attitude – given authority by Locke, Berkeley and Hume and dominant ever since Francis Bacon's formulation of it – encourages a love of facts, evidence, and being practical, which is combined with an open-minded pleasure to be sought from innovation, experimentation and novelty... all very different from that other equally powerful cultural prerogative, the rationalist European tradition, which places the priority on thinking it through before acting and demands theoretical prescriptions first and actions second.' (*UIA International Architect* issue 5)

As editors, we cannot escape our Anglo-Saxon heritage. While admiring the rationalist European approach where practice appears to arise out of theory, we are drawn to a more empirical view of architecture in which theory follows practice.

Editors of magazines are at the forefront in refining, focusing and disseminating ideas. Yet it would be presumptuous and probably incorrect to suggest that shifts and developments in architectural discourse begin as ideas expressed in magazines or books. For us, most good architectural ideas start as buildings, and critics then talk about them. It's not the other way around. We see our editorial role as making sense of what has already been built, in the belief or hope that in the next iteration the design ideas will both evolve and become culturally embedded and accepted.

Architectural design is, intrinsically, a form of research. What distinguishes architectural design research from science-based research is that in science, hypotheses can be tested and the results measured. But architecture is a cultural activity and its ideas can only be tested and find social acceptance through the making of buildings, necessarily many buildings.

We reflect on a time when the finest minds in English-speaking architectural thinking included Colin Rowe, Alison and Peter Smithson, Cedric Price, Alan Colquhoun, Kenneth Frampton, Roy Landau, Joseph Rykwert, Robin Evans: all were contributors to the intellectual life of the AA and beyond, and had been practising architects.

Although we accept these figures now (as then) as significant theoreticians, their work was widely read by practising architects. There is good reason for this. While the methodologies were occasionally influenced by associations with art historians and philosophers, their thinking never strayed far from the reality of practice. The architectural ideas they developed were directly connected to what and how architects design and build.

Who writes to practising architects now?

We consider our editorial role is to present architecture plainly and concisely, not to fly kites. We avoid the esoteric, the pitfall of counting angels on pinheads and the borrowing of critical models from discourses outside architecture. That is why we concentrate exclusively on buildings.

The End of The Architectural Magazine?

Perhaps the end of conventional architectural magazine publishing approaches? Consider: in the 1950s and 60s, a handful of architectural magazines spoke every month to most of the architectural world. In the 1960s, even in outposts like Australia, many offices subscribed to *AD*, *AR*, *Architectural Record, AJ, Domus, JA, PA*. These magazines, based in England, the US, France, Italy, Japan, represented the galaxy of architecture. They were a principal source of design ideas and thinking for architects across the globe.

Today there are numerous text-based architectural journals, written by and published for select readerships within academia. These magazines typically do not reproduce architects' drawings or discuss architects' designs for buildings, the central practice and purpose of architecture. They remain unknown to the majority of architectural practitioners.

About 30 years ago, there was a sudden explosion of architectural publishing. Computerised, high-quality, low-cost offset printing helped; but what ignited the frenzy of architectural publishing that continues was the advent of postmodernism. Two theoretical texts questioning the monolithic direction of modernism – *Complexity and Contradiction in Architecture* by Robert Venturi (1966), and *The Language of Post-Modern Architecture* by Charles Jencks (1977) – made acceptable a pluralist approach to architecture. Suddenly the previously narrow confines of architectural discourse opened onto a broad field upon which any number of architectural positions would be contested.

In this environment, the architectural monograph flourished. Specialist architectural bookshops now exist where architecture books once occupied a few shelves above 'Art'. On display are thousands of titles. All this has been at a price: the progressive collapse of architectural magazine publishing. New magazines continue to spring up, but they are usually flashy, shallow style magazines, semi-technical professional practice magazines, journals of record or academic journals; the first three types are heavily subsidised by advertising by the design manufacturing industry. Many magazines are disposable items to be thumbed through for a quick visual fix and tossed aside when the next issue hits the coffee table in the office reception. Architectural writing in magazines is diminished, degraded into tech-talk, journalese, or made nearly incomprehensible by academics borrowing jargon and concepts from non-architectural discourses.

At the intellectual end of the publishing scale, refereed journals do not speak to practising architects. They mimic literary and scientific journals. The subject matter is typically esoteric and unrelated to architectural practice. The writing is often turgid and the ideas borrowed from non-architectural discourses. Illustrations are secondary to the text. Architects' drawings are nearly non-existent. For a designer, these journals are visually boring, the language hermetic and inaccessible and the topics irrelevant to practice; they are also expensive. These are publications written by academics (and not design academics) for academics; and they are paid for by the academic institutions they are tethered to. Outside academia there is little or no demand for them. Magazines like these turn academic-based architectural thinking into a closed shop that is exiting the orbit of architectural design practice thinking, if it ever was there.

It's a far cry from when Robin Evans or Joseph Rykwert or Richard Padovan were published in an architectural magazine alongside working drawings by Richard Rogers or Mario Botta or Rafael Moneo.

Small Change

Small independent magazines find a place below the radar of commercial and academic publishing, and they do so at considerable cost to their editors. They are like poor theatre: under-funded, passionate, single-minded, precocious, optimistic, creative, spirited, visionary. They are cultural incubators, beacons that can shine a light to show larger, established publications where to go next. Small magazines can afford to be subversive and idiosyncratic, especially if (like *UME*) they don't carry advertising. They have a dispensation to be provocative and edgy (and also to eschew publication schedules).

UME is idiosyncratic but it does not set out to shock, which is not to say that other small magazines shouldn't, and often we are pleased when they do.

We have found there to be a place in architectural discourse for the small magazine that is derrière-garde. UME is comfortable in that role. We always try to envisage where we are going from where we have just been. Thus UME stakes its claim on being the opposite of faddish, fashionable or avant-garde.

What distinguishes all little magazines from commercial and academically funded publications is that they fervently have something to say. But that passion cannot be sustained for very long. And therein lies the crisis that all little magazines must confront. As Peter Eisenman (himself an editor of *Oppositions*, a small magazine) once observed, the best architectural magazines have a life of no more than about eight issues. It takes editors three or four issues to work out what they want to say, and then after three or four more, they usually find they have said it all.

We are aware of this. We have been making architectural magazines for 30 years. The exhaustion of one set of ideas has led us to start new magazines: we left *AD* to launch *International Architect*, and 12 years ago we launched *UME*. *International Architect* went through three editorial adaptations during its 18 issues. *UME* has survived for longer than the statutory eight issues; yet currently, after 21 issues, we are in a hiatus as we take stock to ponder *UME*'s next form as an entirely web-based architectural magazine.

***

November 2010: When we ended our piece, we were in a
state of hiatus while we rethought *UME*'s web-based format.
We can now report that *UME* 22 is in the final stages of
production and will be published on the *UME* website in
early 2011. It is a departure from *UME* 1–21 – and
considerably larger, at 260+ pages: an *oeuvre complète* of the
Brisbane practice of Andresen O'Gorman. *UME* 22 will be
available free online, but also as a limited edition, digitally
printed, loose-leaf boxed set – a return to *UME*'s origins as
a beautiful printed object collected in a box.

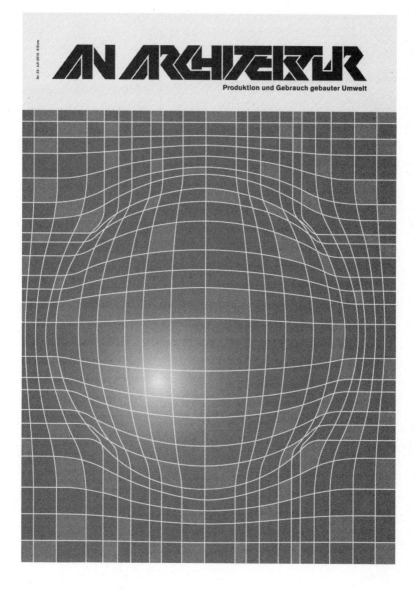

AN ARCHITEKTUR

Produktion und Gebrauch gebauter Umwelt

AN ARCHITEKTUR

Oliver Clemens, Jesko Fezer,
Sabine Horlitz, Anita Kaspar,
Andreas Müller

From the 20 questions put to *An Architektur*, one in particular hit home: 'should there be a purposiveness to architectural writing, which confronts the whimsicality of opinion?' To a certain degree, it is a very wrong question, but, as it touches on an essential misunderstanding, a good point to start. We claim that the assertion that underlies this question – the need to explicitly implement purposiveness in an architectural discourse – is misleading. We would instead ask: 'why the hell does anyone think that the written or spoken word has no purpose or, better still, intention?' Of course there cannot help but be a purposiveness to architectural writing, and so it is troubling to consider that architects often appear reluctant to accept this position. This reluctance further perpetuates a mindset that feeds the ideology of an apolitical discourse. Unfortunately, architectural publishing is usually complicit in propagating such discourse. In this sense, another question must be asked: 'Why does architectural discourse tend to represent itself as non-intentional and non-political?'

Architecture is always framed by certain socio-political principles. While these settings may be privately criticised by some, as a whole the profession generally operates as a service industry to these principles. This is a position that we strongly disagree with. By accepting these socio-political principles as 'reality', architects naively wipe their hands of any social and political responsibility or potentiality. In direct opposition to this, *An Architektur* bases its own practices on a politicised notion of space that regards spatial operations as political acts.

Space as the Site of Social and Political Struggle

Space is never a singular entity, but a multitude of spaces that coexist alongside and influence one another. This networked conception of space characterises the relationships between subject and object, individuals and their built environment. These relationships and their mutual dependencies are socio-spatial constructions, determined as much by hegemonic powers as they are by marginalities and resistance. Space is therefore decidedly political: a construct that is constantly produced and consumed, while being pervaded and claimed by various demands that in turn assume shape and image in space.

Space is a social construct: both product and container of multiple experiences and practices; marked by strategies of power, the contradictions of power logics become tangible experiences, too. Hegemonic forces construct spaces to mediate power into society and structure everyday life and social relations, and also produce experiences of dissent and exclusion. Space can never be neutral. It results from conflicts and negotiations, criss-crossed by antagonisms that expose it to a continuous process of redefinition. Precisely within these moments of negotiation exists the possibility of a political spatial practice.

The Ill-Fated
Tenacity of the Status Quo

To better comprehend the purposiveness of architectural writing – and it matters not whether this purposiveness is explicit or hidden behind a supposed neutrality – two things need to be explored. Firstly, one must find out about the idea of the status quo, the very setting from which an argument is constructed. Secondly, it is helpful to learn about the concept of this intended setting and about its desired state. Both the idea of the status quo and the setting of the intended concept deal with assumptions, imaginations and indeterminate information. Architecture – both its spatial constructions and its written discourses – implicitly deals with these speculations. If purposiveness is the difference between the assumptions of a situation and the ideas of how to improve that situation, then to find out about the purpose of an argument we must necessarily deal with two political issues: the idea of the status of our society and the idea of its potential. That is to say, every text, every statement – whether written, spoken, designed or built – is based upon assumptions about our perceived social reality as well as upon intentions, ambitions and desires related to that.

It is here that the sheer impossibility of 'neutral' architectural writing comes to the fore. Moreover, statements that pretend to be non-intentional frequently hide stronger intentions under layers of feigned objectivity or subjectivity. So why is this subterfuge rarely unmasked? Why does it often seem unnecessary to expose this underlying intentionality? Is it because we are comfortable accepting the status quo and cannot imagine any alternatives to it? Is it that we really believe architecture should only play an affirmative role and therefore ignore any underlying ideological assumptions?

Towards a Politicised Architectural Writing

By contrast, *An Architektur* advocates a wider interpretation of the term architecture. We are concerned with issues of the production and use of built space in general and focus as much on the materiality of space as on the political and social practices that produce space. We therefore understand architecture as a social and political relevant practice. This understanding enables us to be critical of, as well as to suggest claims on architecture that bring a political discourse to the fore. Practically we do not separate the roles of editing, researching, writing and producing a magazine. In this sense, *An Architektur* is an openly structured research team that frequently invites other groups and individuals to cooperate on specific issues. Since these issues are developed within a collective framework, we do not practise the classical division between author and editor.

As editors, architects and researchers we work on architectural topics that we regard as politically relevant: the economy of design; migration and border geographies; oppositional architecture; militarisation of space; advocacy planning; spaces of community; the spatial impacts of globalisation; critical theory and radical geography; segregation by design. Our editorial work centres strongly on questions concerning the purpose of architecture and the intentionality of design. We are convinced that these are political questions – relevant, but rarely posed.

Volume

Archis 2006 #4
Per issue € 17.50, DKK 150, SEK 170, £ 10,
$ 19.95 (USA), $ 22.95 (Canada)
Volume is a project by Archis + AMO + C-LAB + …

Archis

Agitation!
See What Architecture is Shaking

VOLUME

Jeffrey Inaba

On Editing and Writing

1. One thing about editing I've learned over the years is how to quickly assess a publication. Every so often you'll see a person who works in print take hold of a magazine and flip through it. They'll put their thumb on the open face edge and let the pages roll by faster than it's possible to read a page; they'll repeat it a few times and even reverse direction, starting at the back and flipping forward. I used to think this was done out of low regard for the publication since it's not actually being carefully read. But there is a reason for it. It's a good way to understand its editorial sensibility. By flipping the pages it's possible to see the logic of its structure, its hierarchy, sequence of content and design.

2. I disagree with the idea that editing is a different beast than writing. Admittedly, writing is different from editing in that the author(s) produces the entire content of the book, however as forms of expression they bear key similarities. Just as with writing, editing is a way to construct an argument: to make a proposition, reinforce and expand upon it, and draw insights and reflections from it. Editing an issue isn't just about finetuning each author's text or presenting a balanced picture or a comprehensive overview of a subject. Like an authored book, a magazine issue ought to stand on its own based on the integrity of its argumentation, or how well its

story holds together in reasoning and development. Only unlike writing, editing uses numerous people's contributions that come in a variety of formats to construct the story, including multiple text genres, illustrations and pictures. In addition to editing each individual piece to stand as a coherent work with a conceptual wholeness of its own, editing involves composing these pieces to create a single work that serves as a cohesive plotline larger than the sum of the issue's individual parts. While we associate editing with the clarification of material, editing is about amplification – about cumulatively building the sense and effect of a chosen message based upon these autonomous parts.

3. There is some truth to the idea that since the pages of a magazine can be viewed in a random order and not just linearly from front to back, the logic of the argument may not be immediately apparent. But if a publication is done well, the reader will see that editing occurs at multiple levels with small- as well as large-scale interventions. Within the span of just a few pages an editor can create local relationships such as thematic correspondences between contributions. It's satisfying when a magazine has both a larger arc of information that explains the issue more generally and this fine grain arrangement of content throughout the issue that lays out the specific terms of a debate and disagreements among experts.

4. The writing an editor does for his/her publication differs from writing a book or essay by being atmospheric. It doesn't happen in one location as a single continuous text. It is distributed throughout the issue as an ambient texture of information that establishes the reading environment. When successful it doesn't focus attention on

itself but sets the conceptual temperature for reading the featured pieces by functioning as background element recessed from the essays and interviews. These include the editorial, introductions, captions, 'pulled' or emphasised quotes, annotations and titling. Editorial writing is prefatory in that it qualifies what is said in the contribution to familiarise the reader with the claims that follow. At the same time, it is speculative, introducing lines of thought that exceed those offered by the contribution text.

5. From the standpoint of developing an editorial voice for a magazine, discipline goes further than diversity: it's useful to operate within a defined sphere of knowledge and to develop expertise in this limited area of analysis and presentation of content. Within this self-imposed narrow scope it's incumbent on the editors to find surprising information that enriches the mental space of their audience.

6. *Volume*'s editorial team is distributed. *Archis*, AMO and C-Lab take turns assuming the lead for editing an issue. Of course, this is unique for a magazine. We don't work in the same space making a joint decision about every part of every issue. One group will start by determining the theme and key contributors to the issue. When a group isn't taking the lead, they'll act as contributors or advisors. Arjen Oosterman is the editor-in-chief. When he isn't leading the *Archis* issues, he's coordinating the production of the ones led by AMO or C-Lab.

7. I don't think there is an expectation with our readers that there be a consistent editorial voice among the three partners to present a similar perspective from issue to issue. There is instead an interest in the dialogue among editors, an anticipation of what the next theme will be

and how it evolves the editorial discussion, and an interest in the design and presentation of new material. The tag team approach of one group assuming the editorial lead allows each group to intellectually refresh before developing a future issue for our quarterly calendar. It creates an alternation to the magazine that becomes its own unique rhythm of unfolding content. There's a shared commitment to consider the discipline on an international scale, which I would say is *Volume*'s editorial glue, while the alternation enriches its reflexivity. It would be even stronger if we could make it more of a discussion by having a greater number of people guest edit.

8. And within any one issue it doesn't mean everything then has to be presented in a consistent narrative tone. Editing involves ventriloquism – knowing how to communicate with different voices. *Alibi* is one way we do that at *Volume*. It's a magazine within a magazine that appears every so often. It is another way we present studies of urbanisation, in this case through the guidebook genre. We use this voice to introduce urban information through the qualities of the place that are most poignantly understood when experienced in person. As GIS-based analysis justifiably becomes a greater determining factor of planning decisions, we want to reinforce the importance of empirical data to these analyses. In this sense, *Alibi* would be an example of adopting a form or genre to suit an editorial objective. Under the assumed identity of a guidebook, it presents what we believe are important urban processes that are appreciated through firsthand contact: how a city's infrastructure, such as its utility or transportation system, works or doesn't work; and how its human systems support or degrade an area's hydrology,

topography and microclimate. We've done issues on Rio de Janeiro, Kazakhstan's capital Almaty, as well as one on Isle de San Cristobal de Groüt, a fictional condensation of the energy, resource management and planning challenges faced by urbanised islands around the world.

On Form

9. Editing an architecture publication is a unique practice within the discipline because it is a pure operation of content and form. The editor interacts in an immediate way with the information and design – there's no translation of meaning into the form of a building or drawing, for example. It's productive to distinguish between the two to appreciate the fact that the editor can play one off against the other, experimenting with the complexity their relationship can have. There's no need for them to be in agreement or mutually reinforcing in a predictable way, and in fact, the drama of a publication can stem from the incidents of tension between them. Most important to keep in mind is that the narrative is a matter of content and the structure is one of form. The narrative is the storyline that bridges from the beginning to the end of the issue, whereas the structure is the issue's formal framework. The generic magazine structure includes the front matter, which is the introduction, masthead, regularly repeating sections like news and topic-based columns; a feature well with longer, typically commissioned works; and a back matter section with short editorial pieces like reviews, along with credits, etc. Generally speaking, the structure exists independently of the content that goes into it: the same structure can be used from issue to issue with the content fashioned into the pre-defined sections and formats.

10. No, that's not at all the case with *Volume*: it doesn't have a given structure. Every issue is more like a one-off publication in that we take a unique approach to its organisation. We start from scratch with no preconception of what the form will be. For instance, it could be structured into sections of independent unrelated formats, be made entirely of one type of contribution (eg, just images), use a page size that differs from previous issues, have an enlarged amount of supplementary material and reduced amount in the magazine body, or do away with structure *per se* by having all the pieces run as a single continuous document – each of which we've done in the past.

11. Yes, editorial sensibilities vary from magazine to magazine. With *Volume* we are proactive about developing formal strategies to present the content. We invest a lot of time formally calibrating the issue through weighting, pacing and juxtaposition. We establish the overall weighting by positioning at key junctures the texts that are crucial from a polemical standpoint, using them as a nexus around which to locate other pieces (which are essential for their comprehensive treatment, in-depth quantitative analysis or meticulous historical research, among other things). We test the pacing by distributing the contributions by format types, creating alternating patterns by the distances between the same forms, lengthening or shortening the period of their frequency or collapsing it all together. We try to also insert instances of interference by dropping in a piece that is a typological non sequitur in the context of the surrounding contributions, but hopefully suggests a new way of looking at the work itself and the material around it.

12. There are specific formal requirements in publishing. They demand editing with discipline. I like the fact that dimensions are a constraint. We embrace the financial realities of a magazine that necessitate a fixed page count: it cannot be over or under a set number. Everything has to be done within these limits. They determine how much material will go in and the relative density, scale and location of each item. It is a formal limit that defines the editorial content in as much as it forces decisions about hierarchy, emphasis and scope.

13. Maybe the best way to put it is that the editors of *Volume* have a high regard for discipline and an equal amount of suspicion for formulas. Just as there isn't a fixed structure, there isn't a fixed layout. There are some common elements from issue to issue but they are few. We are very fortunate to have Irma Boom as our designer. She and her staff create a new layout every time. Irma's involvement represents the final phase in the editing process. It is the period where we test different kinds of relationships between the narrative and formal organisation through graphic options using colour, typography, image composition and orientation, layout grids, etc. Looking at all the issues of *Volume* side by side shows just how prolific Irma has been in trying a range of treatments in concert with the given themes.

About C-Lab Features and Interviews

14. We produce feature contributions to establish an overview of the topic's urban and architectural implications. Together, the features attempt to construct a provisional topography of the knowledge economy. As part of an

information-based world we are faced with having to assess phenomena that are not historically comparable. Some parameters are qualitative in nature, such as cultural value, social effect and aesthetics, while others are quantifiable in nature, such as technological, economic and environmental influences. The features try to weigh their different impacts on urbanism and architecture and translate them into a common language of effect, which in our case is their impact on the use of spaces.

15. Of course, the more extensive the data, the better the outcome of the analysis. But in many cases this doesn't mean needing access to special sources. The notion of research being amateurish because the data is sourced in the public domain is a misconception. There are plenty of good publicly available data and the amount is increasing as municipalities and states see the benefits of providing metadata for grassroots-initiated urban improvements. It's a matter of having the expertise to find good sources and, more importantly, to know what do with the information: the question is not 'Where does the data come from?' but rather, 'Who has the combined creative and analytical skills to be able to identify informative patterns of use, settlement and exchange that can be the basis for projects that benefit the public realm?' With *Volume* we are further interested in how best to communicate our findings in the features. We spend a lot of time working internally and in consultation with graphic designers to make their implications immediately apparent.

16. Interviews are indeed an ideal format for us because they provide access to the interviewee's obsessions. It can present what is on their mind, what they are currently focused on and how they confront the subject. I say

obsessions, because one can get a glimpse of not just what the interviewee is thinking about, but also how she or he thinks – how he or she processes information and connects thoughts about the topic at hand. Interviews also function as a feedback mechanism for the shaping of the editorial outlook. They help us to learn about a given subject matter and to confirm or reconsider our hypotheses about it.

17. It's the responsibility of the interviewer to orchestrate the exchange by providing the interviewee with a discursive context for the discussion, and to provide direction so that the interviewee knows where the conversation is going (the topics to be addressed, how they relate to one another and the rationale for the particular sequence of questions). A good interviewer also works interactively with the interviewee to improvise and develop what will ultimately become the published content. This happens by asking follow-up questions for the sake of further elaboration, departing from the prepared questions when added layers of related information are needed and deciding when to ask a question that loops back to earlier comments to constellate disparate points of the conversation.

18. After the interview it's necessary to switch gears and to then compose the raw text. Some people are preternaturally gifted with the ability to talk in complete thoughts over the course of what amount to be several paragraphs; but most of us aren't. Typically we reorganise the transcribed text to the extent that the structure of the final printed interview only materialises during this editing process. It's here where the narrative arc is established. Constructing it involves consolidating dialogue when an interviewee discusses the same subject at different times during the discussion, moving a segment so it

lends crucial lead-in background to a statement, or stitching together conversations so they give a fuller perspective as a developed sequence. It's akin to writing insofar as one develops a narrative based upon the selection and ordering of information, only here the information is passages from the transcript.

Beyond the Magazine

19. We do produce other projects besides *Volume*. We have made installations like *Donor Hall* which is at the New Museum; a meditation on suburbia called *Trash* shown at the Walker Art Center; an unofficial materials collection of the Breuer building for the Whitney Museum of American Art, and now we're doing an animation on weather for an upcoming group show. Some of the other publications we've done include a bootleg edition of *Urban China* magazine and a book with Lars Müller Publishers called *World of Giving*. We like working in other media as well as print, though they are definitely influenced by our print work. Regardless of the medium, we use 2D design elements like illustration, text and annotation to compose graphic surfaces – a technique we've refined through the work on *Volume*.

20. We are now in the business of producing content and not only in the business of producing a print magazine. But there isn't a definitive path magazines should take in broadcasting, since as a discipline I think we have yet to fully appreciate our capacity to translate content into media such as websites, etc. The ones that are doing well started off as websites, like Archinect, BLDGBLOG, Dezeen, We Make Money Not Art, Arch Daily, Architizer. They weren't magazines that migrated over to web-based

publishing. While there is a lot of room to introduce architectural content, I wonder if the long-term potential lies in the territory of form, specifically, how well we edit using the formal elements of the medium. Similar to print editing, online editing tools are relatively straightforward, limited and easy to use. From this finite set the repertoire of techniques is great and it's a matter of how creatively the editing is done: how well it directs the viewer by structuring the information, how fast it works, how thoughtfully content is provided to users. You can see that when you just start clicking away at its internal links, browsing faster than you can really read anything, getting a sense of its organisation, just like flipping.

HUNCH

Salomon Frausto

The architecture journal is a space of architectural thinking – a site that constructs critical dialogue and debate. In particular, the academically oriented architecture journal plays a significant role in shaping architectural thought and discourse. It features fresh and innovative ideas related to the past and present of the built environment.

Since 1999 *Hunch* has presented the conversations taking place within the walls of the Berlage Institute to an international audience. The editorial intention of the journal has been to reflect more precisely on the socio-political issues of the physical world, while at the same time broadening architectural discourse. *Hunch* expands and complements the institute's architectural-urban activities. It is inspired by the intense collaboration between the institute's international community of invited lecturers, guest critics, educational staff, alumni, and postgraduate and doctoral researchers, and is fostered by its research programme and public programme of events and exhibitions. *Hunch* is the exchange platform for linking the Berlage Institute to outside issues and debates. It focuses on the evolving professions of architecture and urbanism and their intersection with contemporary culture, aiming to break down boundaries between architecture and other disciplines, between popular and academic scenes, and between theoretical and professional sectors.

The editorial aim of *Hunch* is to intersect scholarship and professional expertise, providing readers with awareness about the design and realisation of built form while at the same time allowing them to discover relevant and innovative

213

architectural discourse that may propel the cultural and professional aspects of architectural production. Each issue is editorially framed to examine worldwide issues and ideas shaping the built environment in order to rethink the spatial transformations ushered in by globalisation and accelerated by rapid technological change. Topics are selected that are thought to stimulate social, political and cultural dialogue relevant to the construction of the contemporary built environment.

In today's media-saturated world, it has become pertinent for institutions like the Berlage Institute to have a journal that represents not only the culture of the place and time but to also be the bearer of responsibility to frame substantive and constructive dialogue related to the contemporary built environment. New digital technologies have allowed architecture-related discourse to take place quickly online, on blogs and on websites; they have also enabled easier and faster printing, leading to a proliferation of publications on architecture and urbanism. Now more than ever, it has become crucial to give readers an editorially distilled and directed publication.

***

From 1990 to 1999, the Berlage Institute communicated its activities through two major publications. The first, entitled *The Berlage Papers*, was a newsletter containing organisational information, the latest news, vignettes of studio work and lecture announcements. The second was *The Berlage Cahiers*, an annual review of postgraduate student work, which documented one academic year and featured exemplary work from design studios and complementary courses like seminars and master classes. Under the deanship of Wiel Arets, the decision was made to combine the information found in both publications as well as to showcase the rich content presented in select lectures and public events into a single journal. The aim was to move away from a student-oriented publication and to create instead a publication that had an international relevance and perspective based on the discussion that was taking place at the institute. As Arets would write in the autumn of 1999, the goal was to establish 'a new approach – one that attempts to reach a diverse audience; one that demonstrates architecture's true multidisciplinary character; and finally one that we hope will reflect the depth, the originality and of course the difference of ideas, visions and perceptions at the Berlage Institute'.

The editor of *S,M,L,XL*, Jennifer Sigler, was hired to conceive and edit a journal that would eventually become *Hunch*. She served as the founding editor and was responsible for the first six issues, the last of which was a double number. It was at her insistence that the journal was named *Hunch*, evoking 'the beginning of an idea…[the] impetus to define and solve a certain mystery'. Similar to other publications of the late 1990s, the format of *Hunch* was envisaged to have different types of text that each reflected the multivalent aspects of the Berlage Institute. Set within the novel trim size of the width of a novel and the height of a magazine, each issue was unthemed and contained a diary entry, a transcribed lecture, an interview, a theory component, a building project, a photographic essay and other material. Features like the diary entry continued from one issue to the next, providing continuity between issues.

With the issue numbered six and seven, two major shifts occurred – coincidentally in conjunction with the change in deanship from Arets to Alejandro Zaera-Polo. The journal went from being published and distributed in-house to being professionally managed by the now defunct Rotterdam-based Episode Publishers. This double-issue was also the first themed issue, a *liber amicorum* exploring the future role of the architect in society, based on a symposium marking the end of Arets's seven years as dean and the beginning of Zaera-Polo's tenure.

The next four issues were guest edited by Penelope Dean, an alumna of the institute's postgraduate programme and at the time a doctoral student at the University of California, Los Angeles, who travelled between the United States and the Netherlands to edit each issue. Her first issue would present a selection of research, developed at the end of Arets's deanship, dealing with Dutch architecture and urbanism in addition to other material. The remaining three issues under her editorship, the last released in the winter of 2007, would be based directly on three lecture series curated by Zaera-Polo. Each number would follow its own specific structure in an effort to tie different elements together.

The journal then lay dormant for two years while a new publishing partnership was established with NAi Publishers and a new, Netherlands-based editor was found. This two-year hiatus allowed for a rethinking of how best to reflect the mission of the institute, which had expanded beyond its postgraduate programme to include doctoral studies, more public events such as conferences and symposiums, and activities geared more toward the professional sector.

Besides a new publisher and a new editor, issue twelve saw a significant change in the format and design of *Hunch*. This issue introduced a larger trim size, keeping the height the same as the previous issues but expanding the width to a more generous proportion, more contemporary typography, a consistent structure, and a set length of 176 pages. Still designed to have the sensibility of being part magazine and part book, the journal now has three consistent editorial components. Each issue features a selection of contributions on a featured topic, which is developed by the editor based on the discussions taking place at the institute. These contributions are supplemented by marginalia consisting of annotations, explanatory notes, inventories, short stories and terminology. In addition, each issue also presents 'peripheralia', such as short texts, interviews, design projects, snapshots, by leading and emerging architectural thinkers, which do not fall under the rubric of the featured topic but are still interesting and valuable to publish.

The editorial direction continues to stimulate a charged cross-disciplinary dialogue that relates the socio-political and techno-material determinants of Dutch architecture culture to the contemporary international discourse on architecture, urbanism and landscape. Each issue provides a cross-section of the dialogue occurring in the institute's different programmes while trying to weave together a thoughtful narrative of architectural speculations, critical observations and historical awareness.

✳✳✳

At a time when blogging and social networking overshadow in-depth journalism and long-form writing, when image is privileged over text, and information is relentlessly flashed before our eyes, is there still a place for the architecture journal? Now more than ever before, the power of the architecture journal is needed to nourish contemporary architecture culture and to project it forward. But maybe that's just a hunch.

NEW GEOGRAPHIES

Neyran Turan

Is not love some kind of a cosmic imbalance? I
was always disgusted with this notion of 'I love
the world, I love the universe'. Love for me is an
extreme violent act, it is not 'I love you all'.
It means I pick out something and say I love you
more than anything else. - S Zizek

Be it for a journal, a book or an exhibition, editing is a mode
of curation, a strategic selection and a cosmic imbalance similar to Zizek's description of love. Prolonged with an original
agenda or position, it is an uneasy grouping of material whose
togetherness would otherwise not be visible. Regardless of
the possibility to have diverse ambitions and intentions –
either extracting particular commonalities from the past or
the present to make them symptomatically visible or making
a predefined statement to stimulate future work and discussion – an editorial project's intrinsic inclusiveness remains as
equally important as its radical exclusions. The very nature
of the cosmic (im)balance created between these poles (that of
inclusion and exclusion) determines the particularity of any
editorial or curatorial venture.

Especially for the emergence of a new publication
project – like *New Geographies* – the significance of this
(im)balance as well as its strategic relation to a larger agenda
becomes indispensable. *New Geographies* journal has been
launched very recently with the first issue numbered 'zero',
and with the second titled 'After Zero'. The project started
with discussions among the members of the founding

editorial board – who have been doctoral candidates at the Harvard University Graduate School of Design – around our research topics in contemporary urbanism.[1] For the emergence of the publication, two ideas have stood out as important as they each affected the editorial framework and the strategies of the publication.

The first idea has been the reconsideration of design's agency after more than two decades of seeing architecture and urbanism as the spatial manifestation of globalisation. On the one hand, we have experienced the production and popularity of design in our contemporary culture with iconic landmarks and celebrity architectures. On the other hand, designers have been increasingly compelled to address enquiries (related to infrastructure, ecology, culture, etc), which were previously confined to the domains of other disciplines. As much as seeming beyond the capacities of design, these critical questions have opened up a range of technical, formal and social repertoires for architecture and urbanism. Rather than reacting to a predefined context, with these questions design is bound – and perhaps even empowered – to redefine and shape contexts (where design decisions cannot simply be innocent extensions of externalities). Symptoms and challenges such as these might seem to trigger a quest for the need of interdisciplinary expansion in design; however at a much deeper level, of more immediate relevance is the political and formal significance of that very same empowerment. At this juncture, the journal started as a platform to prompt further discussions on design agency and the role of the designer in our contemporary society in a broader spectrum. Being unfettered by – and uninterested in – dichotomies of naive morality, totalising narratives or cynical

1. *New Geographies* founding editorial board: Gareth Doherty, Rania Ghosn, El Hadi Jazairy, Antonio Petrov, Stephen Ramos, Neyran Turan.

escapism, we have been interested in the idea of agency, a capacity in relation to new techniques and strategies as well as a faculty of acting, power and repositioning within the complex field of cultural production.

In addition to agency, the second important idea for the editorial framework of the *New Geographies* project has been the new scales of context that appear in our contemporary culture, or *the geographic*. Within the last two decades, latent theorisation of the geographic paradigm has emerged as a symptom in architecture and urbanism. With their clear and necessary replacement of postwar contextualisms and an emphasis on scale, a number of different discussions regarding landscape, infrastructure and networks produced various interpretations on the expansion of architectural or urban thinking. These are exemplified, for instance, by explorations of infrastructural/landscape urbanism, territory, infrastructure and transnational polity as well as the pervasive 'design as research/mapping' phenomenon. The impact of these explorations is visible within the design disciplines with key words such as rapid urbanisation, mapping, networks and flows, which have affected the analysis and interpretation of emergent mutations on the spatial and urban dimension. These investigations created the necessary setting – and convincing supporting evidence – for much-needed 'retroactive manifestos' of emerging urban realities; however, they have also brought a sophisticated aestheticisation or seductive exaggeration of facts, combined with an unreceptive attitude towards the abundance of that evidence.

In parallel to these developments, beyond dichotomies of merely pragmatic journalistic reporting or isolated academic enquiry detached from any architectural or urban speculation, *New Geographies* positions itself as an alternative platform for new interactions between critical stance and speculative work. By aiming to create a synthetic platform to bring various formats of rigorous work (academic research, design project presentation, critical reflection, intellectual enquiry or any other hybrid formation) as well as incorporating various fields of enquiry (architecture, landscape, planning, geography, sociology), the journal has aspired to create discussions regarding new linkages between the social and the physical, the form and the context, the very large and the very small.

If the ambition of the first volume of *New Geographies* was to set the terms, lay out the general themes (the changing scale and role of design as well as the synthesising aspect of geography) and bring together various formats of work that share our excitement and criticality, then the second volume points to the challenges and possibilities of a 'zero point' (ie, zero-context, cities from scratch, zero-carbon) in architecture and urbanism, and focuses on the provocations regarding the future, or the After Zero. The idea of an After Zero has been crucial from the very initial stages of the publication's development for two reasons. First, it reflects our ambition to explore the future following the zero condition within the contemporary built environment and society – that is, we see zero as a starting point, as a chance to restart, rather than as a finale. In an era of environmental or economic crises, or crises regarding form and context within the design disciplines, After Zero marks the possibility of rejuvenation regarding the political and formal significance of design. Second, After Zero has acknowledged the future premise of our first *New Geographies* volume AFTER our previous volume, titled ZERO. After previous strategies of wilful reality mapping or iconic formalism, volume 1 has aimed to investigate possibilities after crises, after mapping and after signature architectures.

In his definition for the *Dictionary of Human Geography*, geographer Derek Gregory defines geography as 'earth-writing' through its Greek roots – *geo* (earth) and *graphia* (writing), articulated as writing both on and about the world. Gregory writes:

[T]he practice of making geographies ('geo-
graphing') involves both writing about
(conveying, expressing or representing) the
world and also writing (marking, shaping or
transforming) the world. The two fold in and
out of one another in an ongoing and constantly
changing series of situated practices, and
even when attempts have been made to hold geo-
graphing still, to confine its objects and
methods to a formal discipline, it has always
escaped those enclosures.[2]

Marking a clear interest to see *the geographic* as a much
broader framework for architecture and urbanism rather than
merely a shift in scale, the initial two volumes of the journal
have proposed the idea as a new synthetic ground in terms of
its potential to link physical, political and aesthetic attributes.
Furthermore, in parallel to the double signification inherent
in the idea of geography – both writing *about* (representation,
expression, analysis) and *on* (marking, shaping, transforming)
the earth – the geographic framework was relevant for its
ability to emphasise both the *analysing* and the *shaping* of
the forces that constitute the built environment.

   As a plausible form of 'adaptive reaction' within
a post-crisis society, Anthony Giddens has a renowned
preference for the attitude of radical engagement over the
other possible attitudes he puts forward – pragmatic
acceptance, sustained optimism or cynical pessimism.[3]
Similarly the idea of design agency connotes an inclusive
willingness for understanding and impacting realities.

2. Derek Gregory, 'Geography', *Dictionary of Human Geography* (London:
Blackwell, 2008).
3. Anthony Giddens, *The Consequences of Modernity* (Stanford, CA: Stanford University
Press, 1990), pp 134–37.

However, agency becomes relevant to the extent that it can balance this inclusive attitude with strategic suspensions and necessary exclusions. Thus, while marking an interest to better understand wider contexts/scales and interdisciplinary juxtapositions, design agency equally connotes a strong belief in design's intrinsic specificity, as well as its power to challenge these larger aspects.

As described, geography has been a latent phenomenon in architecture and urbanism, and further explorations are needed to cultivate its potentiality in terms of understanding histories and projecting futures. The inherent potential of the geographic is explored in interesting ways in the disciplines of environmental history and political ecology. Perhaps what is needed more in the design disciplines are rigorous approaches that will go beyond exaggerated depictions of contemporary globalisation, objectified/sophisticated cartographies and fascination with seductive facts, and focus more on the kind of questions and possibilities these facts bring to the table. If the true potentiality of the *geographic* for architecture and urbanism lies in its ability to provide unconventional perspectives and ideas on the political and provisional aspects of our built environment, this enquiry evidently requires a 'radical engagement' in interdisciplinary discussions but, perhaps more importantly, it also calls for a belief in the disciplinary specificities of architecture and urbanism and a willingness to incorporate these discussions into our thinking and practice in unusual ways. In this context, editorial projects like *New Geographies* gain further significance in their capacity to push boundaries and instigate prospective lines of thinking for architecture and urbanism. These editorial projects might not 'love them all', but will certainly continue to create cosmic imbalances and activate design's potential to imagine alternative futures.

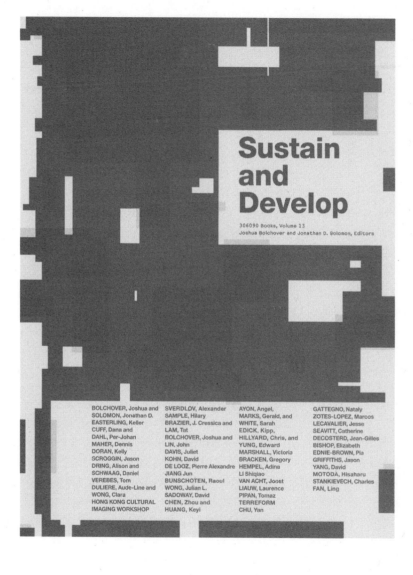

306090

Jonathan D Solomon

In the late spring of 2007, I was sitting in my office grading
undergraduate papers when I noticed an odd trend in a block
of text. Suddenly, midway through a paragraph on water
rights issues, I detected a surprising change in font, leading
and aspect. The architecture students' default Arial Sans
Unicode had given way to Windows default Times New
Roman. Moreover, every tenth word or so was printed in a
deep cobalt blue, and underlined. Interest piqued, I typed
out the suspect paragraph into Google and hit the 'I Feel
Lucky' key. Lo and behold, up popped a Wikipedia page.
To add insult to injury, the student had slapped a superscript
numeral onto this sloppy sampling that referred me to an
endnote reading simply: 'Wikipedia'. So much for my
plagiarism hearing.

Since then I have been tilting at the windmill of
casual sourcing amongst my students, with some positive
effects. But the telltale serifs of that brazen cut-and-paste
appropriation were hints of a deeper and more pressing crisis.
At issue are a range of things, from the academic: the proper
sourcing procedure for a Wikipedia article, the proper uses
of primary, secondary and tertiary sources, to the critical:
the role of searchable, non-hierarchical content-compilers
in academic and professional culture.

Google's 'Don't Sort. Search' is the 'Less is More'
of our time. Through projects such as Google Book Search,
an attempt to create a digitised archive of every book ever
published, this maxim has a resounding effect on how
we organise content both in our daily lives and in our

professional, creative and academic work. Google's book venture has drawn interest in the field of copyright law, where it promises to have the most significant financial impact by upturning traditional limitations on access, although those who actually use the books in question have taken it largely in their stride. Scholars have reacted more aggressively to Wikipedia, which does not simply provide access to knowledge but creates discourse through the establishment of new user-defined content streams. Wikipedia's notion of emergent editing is particularly threatening to those who still believe that discourse is formed by those very hierarchies Wikipedia has reinvented. (In 2007, Jorge Cauz, president of Britannica, told *New Yorker* author Stacey Schiff in an email that without editorial oversight Wikipedia would 'decline into a hulking mediocre mass of uneven, unreliable, and, many times, unreadable articles').

What are our responsibilities as creators of discourse, managers of taste, and trained reviewers in this era? Are traditional hierarchies dead? Be they hierarchies of value, seeking to separate 'good' from 'bad', or of organisation, breaking material down under headings of topic or theme – what should replace them?

Both Flickr, the web-based image-sharing utility, and Wikipedia, the ubiquitous bottom-up encyclopedia, figure largely and positively in my work as an editor. I am struggling to use them as aids to new hierarchies rather than as agents of their elimination. Architecture has always been a profession of sorters and of searchers, what better profession to explore new forms of editing in our new milieu? Google and Wikipedia have proved searching to be extraordinarily powerful. As an architect and an editor I believe in the power of the sort as well. In fact, we must become comfortable and facile with both; a new maxim – 'Search, Sort, Search, Sort – governs our way forward.

The following chain of choice begins with the first paragraph of the Wikipedia entry for 'Theme' and follows it through a selection from the first available links to a proceeding entry 20 times to end at the entry on 'Critical Thinking'. Each paragraph is illustrated with an image found on the first page of a search under the same field of the Creative Commons licensed material on Flickr.

1. A **theme**, from Old French *tesme*, is a broad idea in a story or literary work, or a message or lesson conveyed by a written text. This message is usually about **life**, society or human nature. Themes often explore timeless and universal ideas. Most themes are implied rather than explicitly stated. The theme is different from the superficial outlay of the text; it is normally the meaning of the text on a deeper, more abstract level.[1]

Image: Santa Cruz Boardwalk – Theme Park. The mini theme park at the Santa Cruz boardwalk. By compujeramy. <http://www.flickr.com/ photos/compujeramey/ 10775576/>.

2. **Life** is a state that distinguishes organisms from non-living objects, such as non-live, and dead organisms, being manifested by growth through **metabolism** and reproduction. Some living things can communicate and many can adapt to their environment through changes originating internally. A physical characteristic of life is that it feeds on negative entropy. In more detail, according to physicists such as John Bernal, Erwin Schrödinger, Eugene Wigner, and John Avery, life is a member of the class of

1. Theme (Literature). Wikipedia, The Free Encyclopedia. 30 September 2008, 00:38 UTC. Wikimedia Foundation Inc, 30 September 2008 <http://en.wikipedia.org/wiki/ Theme_(literature)>.

1

2

3

4

5

6

7

8

phenomena which are open or continuous systems able to decrease their internal entropy at the expense of substances or free energy taken in from the environment and subsequently rejected in a degraded form (see: entropy and life).[2]

Image: paper-life – give her your heart. paper-life – dê-lhe o seu coração. By *madalena-pestana*. <http://www.flickr.com/photos/madalena_pestana/2112973208/>.

3. **Metabolism** is the set of **chemical reactions** that occur in living organisms in order to maintain life. These processes allow organisms to grow and reproduce, maintain their structures, and respond to their environments. Metabolism is usually divided into two categories. Catabolism breaks down organic matter, for example to harvest energy in cellular respiration. Anab-

olism, on the other hand, uses energy to construct components of cells such as proteins and nucleic acids.[3]

Image: 黒川紀章・中銀カプセルタワービル *Nakagin Capsule Tower, Tokyo, Kisho Kurokawa. By pict_u_re. <http://www.flickr.com/photos/pict_u_re/1575994789/>.*

4. A **chemical reaction** is a process that always results in the interconversion of **chemical substances**. The substance or substances initially involved in a chemical reaction are called reactants. Chemical reactions are usually characterised by a chemical change, and they yield one or more products, which are in general different from the reactants. Classically, chemical reactions encompass changes that strictly involve the motion of electrons in the forming and breaking of

2. Life. Wikipedia, The Free Encyclopedia. 10 September 2008, 4:54 UTC. Wikimedia Foundation Inc, 30 September 2008 < http://en.wikipedia.org/wiki/Life >.
3. Metabolism. Wikipedia, The Free Encyclopedia. 27 September 2008, 16:46 UTC. Wikimedia Foundation Inc, 30 Sept 2008. <http://en.wikipedia.org/wiki/Metabolism>.

chemical bonds, although the general concept of a chemical reaction, in particular the notion of a chemical equation, is applicable to transformations of elementary particles, as well as nuclear reactions.[4]

Image: Airbox. The airbox is fed by two intake pipes that are located on the nose. Like two nostrils they suck in air necessary for the chemical reaction that converts potential energy to kinetic. Each cylinder has its own throttle body and injector. Everything is designed to flow the maximum amount of gas. By k.ivoutin. <http://www.flickr.com/photos/ivoutin/1523518450/>.

5. A **chemical substance** is a **material** with a definite chemical composition. It is a concept that became firmly established in the late eighteenth century after work by the chemist Joseph Proust on the composition of some pure chemical compounds such as basic copper carbonate. He deduced that, 'All samples of a compound have the same composition; that is, all samples have the same proportions, by mass, of the elements present in the compound'. This is now known as the law of constant composition. Later with the advancement of methods for chemical synthesis particularly in the realm of organic chemistry; the discovery of many more chemical elements and new techniques in the realm of analytical chemistry used for isolation and purification of elements and compounds from chemicals that led to the establishment of modern chemistry, the concept was defined as is found in most chemistry textbooks. However, there are some controversies regarding this definition mainly because

4. Chemical Reaction. Wikipedia, The Free Encyclopedia. 30 September 2008, 04:21 UTC. Wikimedia Foundation Inc, 30 September 2008 <http://en.wikipedia.org/wiki/Chemical_reaction>.
5. Chemical Substance. Wikipedia, The Free Encyclopedia. 30 September 2008, 06:28 UTC. Wikimedia Foundation Inc, 30 September 2008 <http://en.wikipedia.org/wiki/Chemical_substance>.

the large number of chemical substances reported in chemistry literature need to be indexed.[5]

Image: Chemical Substances Storage Room at Killing Fields, Phnom Penh, Cambodia By alex.ch. <http:// www.flickr.com/photos/alex-photos/408905773/>.

6. **Materials** are physical **substances** used as inputs to production or manufacturing. Raw materials are first extracted or harvested from the earth and divided into a form that can be easily transported and stored, then processed to produce semi-finished materials. These can be input into a new cycle of production and finishing processes to create finished materials, ready for distribution and consumption.[6]

Image: The Fencing Is Covered With Wrapping Material. Wrapping Material is secured to the box. Fence is inside the wrapping material. Box is inside the fence. Charges are inside the box. By Sister72. <http://www.flickr. com/photos/sis/136233669/>.

7. **Substance** is a 1987 double **compilation album** by New Order, consisting of all of the band's singles at that point in their 12-inch versions, together with their respective B-side tracks. The then newly-released non-album single True Faith is also featured, along with its B-side 1963. The collection was released on vinyl, double CD, double cassette and Digital Audio Tape.[7]

Image: Substance. By b.schrade. <http:// www.flickr.com/ photos/13655232@ N03/2781476928/>.

6. Material. Wikipedia, The Free Encyclopedia. 29 September 2008, 20:37 UTC. Wikimedia Foundation Inc, 30 September 2008 <http://en.wikipedia.org/wiki/Material>.
7. Substance (New Order Album). Wikipedia, The Free Encyclopedia. 28 September 2008, 22:48 UTC. Wikimedia Foundation Inc, 30 September 2008 <http://en.wikipedia. org/wiki/Substance_(New_Order_album)>.

8. A **compilation album** is an album (music or spoken-word) featuring tracks from one or multiple recording artists, often culled from a variety of sources (such as **studio albums**, live albums, singles, demos and outtakes.) The tracks are usually collected according to a common characteristic, such as popularity, source or subject matter. When the tracks are all essentially by the same recording artist, a *compilation album* is often referred to as a retrospective album. Compilation albums may employ traditional product bundling.[8]

Image: Olongapo City Album. Compilation of selected photos ... all taken by me through my Canon Powershot and N70 Cameraphone. By tolitzdelacasa. <http://www. flickr.com/photos/matang_ agila/217697938/>.

9. A **studio album** is an original collection of new tracks by a recording artist. It usually does not contain live recordings and/or remixes, and if it does, those tracks do not make up a majority of the album and are often called bonus tracks. Due to their lightly prepared nature, they can contain a variety of flourishes and production techniques, including **segues**, sound effects, found sound, and band contributions.[9]

Image: IMG_8841. By eyeliam. <http://www.flickr.com/photos/ eyeliam/2708337288/>.

10. The **Segway PT** is a two-wheeled, self-balancing electric vehicle invented by Dean Kamen. It is produced by Segway Inc. of New Hampshire, USA. The name Segway is a **homophone** of segue (a smooth transition,

8. Compilation Album. Wikipedia, The Free Encyclopedia. 24 September 2008, 09:32 UTC. Wikimedia Foundation Inc, 30 September 2008 <http://en.wikipedia.org/wiki/ Compilation_album>.
9. Studio Album. Wikipedia, The Free Encyclopedia. 11 September 2008, 05:05 UTC. Wikimedia Foundation Inc, 30 September 2008 <http://en.wikipedia.org/wiki/Studio_ album>.

9

10

11

12

13

14

15

16

literally Italian for 'follows').
PT is an initialism for
personal transporter while
the old suffix *HT* was
an initialism for *human
transporter.*[10]

*Image: segue II. By striatic.
<http://www.flickr.com/
photos/striatic/2489578182/>.*

11. A **homophone** is a word
that is pronounced the same
as another word but differs in
meaning. The words may be
spelled the same, such as *rose*
(flower) and *rose* (past tense
of rise), or differently, such
as *carat*, *caret*, and *carrot*,
or *two* and *too*, or *know* and
no. A homophone is a type of
homonym, although some-
times *homonym* is used to
refer only to homophones that
have the same spelling but
different meanings. The term
may also be used to apply
to units shorter than words,
such as letters or groups of

letters that are pronounced
the same as another letter or
group of letters.[11]

*Image: ecce homo.
By jkido-san.
<http://www.flickr.com/
photos/jikido/192944380/>.*

12. A **rose** is a perennial
flowering shrub or vine
of the **genus** *Rosa*, within
the family Rosaceae, that
contains over 100 species.
The species form a group of
erect shrubs, and climbing
or trailing plants, with
stems that are often armed
with sharp thorns. Most are
native to Asia, with smaller
numbers of species native to
Europe, North America, and
northwest Africa. Natives,
cultivars and hybrids are
all widely grown for their
beauty and fragrance.[12]

*Image: a lonely rose...
Roses are always beautiful.*

10. Segue PT. Wikipedia, The Free Encyclopedia. 26 September 2008, 02:59 UTC. Wikimedia Foundation Inc, 30 Sept 2008. <http://en.wikipedia.org/wiki/Segue_PT>.
11. Homophone. Wikipedia, The Free Encyclopedia. 29 September 2008, 20:16 UTC. Wikimedia Foundation Inc, 30 Sept 2008. <http://en.wikipedia.org/wiki/Homophone>.
12. Rose. Wikipedia, The Free Encyclopedia. 27 September 2008, 15:05 UTC. Wikimedia Foundation Inc, 30 Sept 2008. <http://en.wikipedia.org/wiki/Rose>.

13. A **genus** (plural: genera, from Greek: Γένος; Latin genus 'descent, family, type, gender') is a low-level **taxonomic** rank used in the classification of living and fossil organisms. The taxonomic ranks are life, domain, kingdom (biology), phylum, class (biology), order (biology), family (biology), genus, and species[13]

Image: Wallaby Stood there for 20 minutes while I took photos about 5M away. Wallabia bicolor (note the American spelling in the obviously Australian-based Latin species name). Scientific nomenclature seems to follow its own rules! The Swamp Wallaby is the only living member of the Genus Wallabia having different genetic, dental, reproductive and behavioural characteristics to other Wallabies in the genus Macropus. By wollombi.

14. **Taxonomy** is the practice and science of classification. The word comes from the Greek τάξις, taxis (meaning 'order', 'arrangement') and νόμος, nomos ('law' or 'science'). Taxonomies, or taxonomic schemes, are composed of *taxonomic units* known as *taxa* (singular *taxon*), or kinds of things that are arranged frequently in a **hierarchical** structure. Typically they are related by subtype-supertype relationships, also called parent-child relationships. In such a subtype-supertype relationship the subtype kind of thing has by definition the same constraints as the supertype kind of thing plus one or more additional constraints. For example, car is a subtype of vehicle. So any car is also a vehicle,

13. Genus. Wikipedia, The Free Encyclopedia. 28 September 2008, 16:12 UTC. Wikimedia Foundation Inc, 30 September 2008 <http://en.wikipedia.org/wiki/Genus>.

17

18

19

20

but not every vehicle is a car. Therefore, a thing needs to satisfy more constraints to be a car than to be a vehicle.[14]

Image: Coruja-buraqueira (Speotyto cunicularia) assustada 65 20–09–07 030. By Flávio Cruvinel Brandão. <http://www.flickr.com/ photos/flaviocb/1414267073/>.

15. A **hierarchy** is an arrangement of objects, people, elements, values, grades, orders, classes, etc., in a **ranked** or graduated series. The word derives from the Greek ιεραρχία (hierarchia), from ιεράρχης (hierarches), 'president of sacred rites, high-priest' and that from ιερός (hieros), 'sacred' + ἄρχω (arkho), 'to lead, to rule'.

14. Taxonomy. Wikipedia, The Free Encyclopedia. 29 September 2008, 18:38 UTC. Wikimedia Foundation Inc, 30 September 2008 <http://en.wikipedia.org/wiki/Taxonomy>.

The word can also refer to a series of such items so arranged. Items in a hierarchy are typically thought of as being above, below, or at the same level as one another.[15]

Image: Hierarchy. you got to know your place, being a chicken. By hans_s. <http://www.flickr.com/photos/archeon/23558506/>.

16. Academic organisations typically have a rather rigid set of **ranks**. Those listed below refer specifically to **universities**, although colleges and other institutions may follow a similar schema.[16]

Image: East Blue – Trendy mall with ranking system [Blue Ravine]. Future Create City [Blue Ravine] is a shopping mall equipped with Sales distribution + ranking + sales support synchronisation system. Ranking board

installation to understand trend at one view. fashion, shop,high,quality,mall,desi gn,skin. By Torley. <http://www.flickr.com/photos/torley/2610133706/>.

17. A **university** is an institution of higher education and **research**, which grants academic degrees in a variety of subjects. A university provides both undergraduate education and postgraduate education. The word *university* is derived from the Latin *universitas magistrorum et scholarium*, roughly meaning 'community of teachers and scholars'.[17]

Image: Moscow State Univeristy. This is an HDR image constructed from three different raw files using Photomatix. By Eldar. <http://www.flickr.com/photos/eldar/141207847/>.

15. Hierarchy. Wikipedia, The Free Encyclopedia. 23 September 2008, 17:08 UTC. Wikimedia Foundation Inc, 30 Sept 2008. <http://en.wikipedia.org/wiki/Hierarchy>.
16. Academic Rank. Wikipedia, The Free Encyclopedia. 29 September 2008, 12:38 UTC. Wikimedia Foundation Inc, 30 Sept 2008. <http://en.wikipedia.org/wiki/Academic_rank>.
17. University. Wikipedia, The Free Encyclopedia. 29 September 2008, 19:46 UTC. Wikimedia Foundation Inc, 30 September 2008 <http://en.wikipedia.org/wiki/University>.

18. **Research** is defined as human activity based on **intellectual** application in the investigation of matter. The primary aim for applied research is discovering, interpreting, and the development of methods and systems for the advancement of human knowledge on a wide variety of scientific matters of our world and the universe. Research can use the scientific method, but need not do so.[18]

Image: Comfortable Research New York City, 2006 – I spotted this room en route to an appointment in the same building. The light, as you can see, was too magnificent to pass by. By Joel Bedford. <http://www. flickr.com/photos/jalex_ photo/397581862/>.

19. An **intellectual** (from the adjective meaning 'involving thought and reason') is a person who tries to use his or her intelligence and **critical** analytical thinking, either in their profession or for the benefit of personal pursuits.[19]

Image: An intellectual Parque Expo, Lisbon, Portugal. By pedrosimoes7. <http:// www.flickr.com/photos/ pedrosimoes7/106326062/>.

20. **Critical thinking** consists of mental processes of discernment, analysis and evaluation. It includes possible processes of reflecting upon a tangible or intangible item in order to form a solid judgment that reconciles scientific evidence with common sense. In contemporary usage 'critical' has a certain negative connotation that does not apply in the present case.[1] Though the term 'analytical thinking' may seem to convey the idea more accurately, critical thinking clearly involves synthesis,

18. Research. Wikipedia, The Free Encyclopedia. 28 September 2008 19:43 UTC. Wikimedia Foundation Inc, 30 September 2008 <http://en.wikipedia.org/wiki/Research>.
19. Intellectual. Wikipedia, The Free Encyclopedia. 29 September 2008, 16:27 UTC. Wikimedia Foundation Inc, 30 September 2008 <http://en.wikipedia.org/wiki/Intellectual>.

evaluation, and reconstruction of thinking, in addition to analysis. Critical thinkers gather information from all senses, verbal and/or written expressions, reflection, observation, experience and reasoning. Critical thinking has its basis in intellectual criteria that go beyond subject-matter divisions and which include: clarity, credibility, accuracy, precision, relevance, depth, breadth, logic, significance and fairness.[20]

Image: Using Second Life's 3D Online World to Train Online Students. Instructional designers and faculty in any educational programme will benefit from this presentation. Included in this presentation is the unveiling of an innovative emergency/ nursing education simulator (NESIM). Live patient simulations will be created and role played while RN student teams use the NESIM simulator to apply critical thinking skills and interventions. By Daneel Ariantho. <http:// www.flickr.com/photos/ daneelariantho/1989039795/>.

20. Critical thinking. Wikipedia, The Free Encyclopedia. 29 September 2008, 21:38 UTC. Wikimedia Foundation Inc, 30 September 2008 <http://en.wikipedia.org/wiki/ Critical_thinking>.

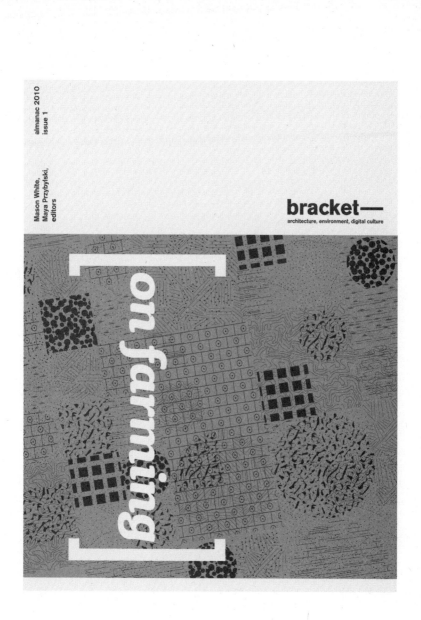

almanac 2010
issue 1

Mason White,
Maya Przybylski,
editors

bracket—
architecture, environment, digital culture

[on farming]

[BRACKET]

Mason White

Confession

Two things are important to state from the outset. One, we have only recently published the first issue; and two, we are not editors, nor do we even like the idea of editors as some evolved and selected disciplinary species. In many ways, as in Roland Barthes' proclamation of the death of the author, our age could be witness to the death of the editor. Just as Barthes preferred the term scriptor over author as a means to subvert the authority embedded in the term, the editor could be said to have lost its status. We for one do not mourn this loss. These days, who isn't an editor in some form or another?

Death of the Editor

Several factors, especially the power and reach of internet platforms, have increasingly threatened the status of the traditional editor, critic and curator. This has yielded two general results: the repositioning of media to embrace new platforms and dissemination methods; and the entrenchment of traditional curatorial and editorial roles. Recognising that the entrenchment of editorial roles is more easily identifiable and familiar, let us look at the phenomenon of new dissemination platforms. A 2009 article in the *New York Times* featured a blogger who runs a site called classymommy. com, which receives about 60,000 visitors each month. Companies in the market sector of children's goods are eager to seek her approval and to have items featured on her site. Yet, this individual has no editor-in-chief and no publisher to oversee and manage content prior to public reading. She sees something she likes and within hours it can be reviewed and then read by a like-minded consumer. The potential of bloggers to elevate or hand-pick an item (or idea) out of the clutter of products (or projects) is immense and can yield highly desired internet chatter. Another case study in point is the music review site based in Chicago called pitchfork.com which maintains some 60 'contributing writers' in addition to about 10 staff writers. With the intention to have albums, videos or singles featured by an editor, their office is flooded as much if not more than a typical radio station. These bloggers are often called influencers. This is the true status of the editor. At *[bracket]* we would be so fortunate that the result of our efforts is that of an influencer, though this is not the origin of our intentions.

Origins

[bracket] emerges out of a collaboration between Archinect, an online community platform for architects and designers established in 1997, and InfraNet Lab, a blog focused on infrastructure, networks and environments established in 2008. The resulting publication is the merger of the personalities and structure of these forums as much as the thematic interests embedded in their content. Yet, in many ways *[bracket]* has created its own identity and sidesteps the difficult challenge of bringing either of these websites into a print medium.

At *[bracket]*, we embrace our amateur status and confess to an *intentionally distracted focus* in our operations. Our interest is focused but is open to unexpected tangents that test the edges of that interest. In short our origins are simple: we do not like the current state of architecture publications and want to make something that we ourselves would be excited to discover. Several publications rely heavily on selling the product by featuring works of writers or designers who are well-known. Not that we have anything against the latest project from Toyo Ito or essay by Peter Eisenman, we just do not feel that as a medium we should be yet another outlet for their dissemination; there are more tried and true outlets for this.

We have settled on the term almanac to describe our format. Journal, magazine, blog and book do not fit, but almanac suggests an annual publication that serves to chart and predict. Similar to the *Farmer's Almanac*, an ongoing publication initiated in 1818 that offered environmental data and weather predictions, *[bracket]* collects information and speculations on present and future environments.

Positioning Content

Our intention is to privilege the positioning of content over the critique of content. Criticality, left to the reader, will emerge from the association and juxtaposition of issues relevant to our primary interests of architecture, environment and digital culture. In fact, *[bracket]* highlights issues rather than specific authors/designers and consciously shies away from the usual suspects.

Opinion is not our agenda. Instead, we foreground an argument that architecture's expanded field necessitates the tabling of new questions from new voices. Given the deluge of information available to designers, readers and writers, we believe that filtering, diverting and collating content, as in the case of influencers of pitchfork or classymommy, is equally important; it is the necessary precursor to opinion.

Themes

Thematic issues, for better or worse, are useful structuring systems for content delivery as they generate a focused response from contributors as well as a common reference and vocabulary for readers. Are non-thematic issues polemically sterile? Hard to say, for what is non-thematic? Everything seems to possess a strand of commonality otherwise it is a Borges Chinese Encyclopaedia, which of course is fascinating but ultimately more novelty than a productive curation.

The larger question here being how can a range of interpretations to a selected theme be achieved without defaulting simply to an architecture *du jour*? Above all, the subject should be timely and maintain its greatest impact upon its release date. This is an accepted fact of our output – that it is timely but exhibits a short shelf life, while perhaps serving the future with the potential to be revisited after some years with the context of the events that followed its release.

Format / Structure

The format is intended to have the structure and feel of a website, but the linearity of a publication. As much as we would like to distance ourselves from traditional editing, ultimately someone has to propel and mobilise the effort. In a way, if we were to be seen as editors, then we are more editors of the structure of the content than the content itself. The hope is that each contributor and reader will themselves be as much an editor as we are, generating a more inclusive form of curation.

[bracket] is organised in an open, multi-tiered way. Each issue is proposed by a different combination of curators,

who establish a theme with its possible misinterpretations, then curate a jury, which serves as a one-off editorial board. This temporary editorial board, which is invested in the theme, provides the experience and knowledge from which projects and texts are selected.

We think this model is more effective than traditional ones, because the 'editorial board' is constantly reshuffling so that *[bracket]* doesn't stagnate, and this also allows for the unexpected. So many editorial models are only interested in selecting content that will sell (eg, a feature on the latest Zaha Hadid project or an essay from an established author); our interest is more about the discovery of emerging or new voices within the field.

Disciplinary Seams

We view our role as educators who reference and cite projects, texts and ideas as a way to provoke students to position their thinking and work relative to the trajectory of ideas. Critiquing the role of the architect is the very foundation of *[bracket]*. Our position is that we are witnesses and chroniclers of an amazing shift from the architect as form-giving innovator to the architect as programmatic innovator – the distinction being that the architect is central to the invention of spatial performances, but form is not always its primary vehicle. Architects need also to confront other issues, such as climate change, resources and threatened ecologies. *[bracket]* seeks out thematics that offer a range of responses across the design disciplines. The hope is that projects and texts will emerge from thinkers who are willing to occupy the seam of design disciplines.

INTERSTICES 07
GEN-IUS/GEN-EALOGY

INTERSTICES

Ross Jenner

The topics which *Interstices: Journal of Architecture and Related Arts*[1] addresses tend to pose questions that are yet to have defined solutions. If a solution to a problem has already been found, there is no need for us to get involved. From the beginning, *Interstices* has been programmatically committed to the unresolved, overlooked, fraught, leftover issues that may require a solution – or indeed, may not.

    Interstices does not set itself up to solve problems. In fact, we often defer and disturb solutions. The introduction to the first issue stated that the journal is not meant 'to reaffirm existing normative standards and canons, nor to rest comfortably in the supposed self-sufficiency of the building object, regional identity, composition, nature, function... but to explore the interstices, the gaps and fractures within an institution that appears solid, secure and fixed'. *Interstices*, as its name suggests, is about 'the spaces between idea and thing where perfect correspondence is never quite found, demanding a realm of endless negotiation and interpretation that we see as productive'.[2] We noted at the time a similar separation to that which Hubert Damisch found in Viollet-le-Duc: 'the "truth" of a building is not to be found in bricks and mortar any more than in the outer form. No, it lies in the space between them, that which makes them complementary, in that space where style is born, in that gap between things

---

1. See also www.interstices.auckland.ac.nz. My thanks to Tina Engels-Schwarzpaul for her invaluable help in preparing this account.
2. Introduction, *Interstices* 01, 1991.

which is intimated in the absence of a logical link...'

The journal, then, was intended as a sounding of the cavities within the walls that sustain architecture. No schema posed in terms of composition, structure or function can any longer adequately cover either the production or the account of the design in hand. With the invasion of language into the problematic of architecture, and without centre, everything becomes susceptible to the play of discourse. Similarly, questions of place, identity, regionalism, post-colonialism, relations between the modern and the non-modern, can only be posed in conjectural terms, constituted by negotiation, splicing, juxtaposition, collage. Cultural factors are seen to be mixed, relational, inventive and mobile. From the start, we also acknowledged that the institutionally defined disciplinary boundaries are being increasingly threatened and crossed. A productive tension has been found in the intervals between architecture and other art forms.

Interstices sprang from a series of annual seminars, aimed initially at increasing consciousness in architectural circles of developments in theory in all disciplines. Unexpectedly, it became a platform the like of which did not seem to exist in the wider university. Therefore, colleagues from other departments became involved early on. The journal was initiated by a postgraduate architecture student, Nigel Ryan, with my support as an academic, and it has since been edited by academics, often with the aid of postgraduate students. Since *Interstices 06*, we have maintained a joint editorship between the University of Auckland and AUT University. The devoted editorship of Tina Engels-Schwarzpaul from the latter has produced a radical revitalisation of the journal in all aspects of its form and content.[3]

Since a forum for such discussion could survive only outside the restrictions of immediate commercial appeal and the simple publicity needed by the architectural profession, *Interstices* and the associated Under Construction Lecture

Series always had to be funded by alternative sources. The New Zealand Arts Council provided grants for the first two or three issues and later, in a loose association, so did the University of Auckland and, later still, AUT University. A publication like *Interstices* needs to maintain its independence in order to preserve the intellectual elbow room needed both for a critical engagement and for editorial decisions. Having said that, we could not survive without the funding made available by the universities on a regular basis, nor without the generous sponsorship of practising architects.

The shift in architectural theory and history in the 1970s and 1980s, from a largely practitioner-based discourse to one led by professional theorists and historians, made necessary the adoption of the sort of scholarly content and critique demonstrated in other academic disciplines to which architecture had to measure up. In this sense, one could say that a professionalisation of historians and theorists in academia led to a transformation of teachers into editors and universities into publishing houses, even though this development was underway quite some time before the initiation of *Interstices*. Academic professionalism has also meant, however, that in recent times in Australasia, as in the UK, publication is now driven by research assessment exercises.[4] For *Interstices*, the demands of such a regime resulted first in the introduction of a refereeing process, and now in the

3. John Walsh commented that *Interstices* prior to the revival had had 'an occurrence so occasional that its status lay somewhere between rumour and secret. If it was a bird, it would have been of some lesser spotted species. But lately, the publication has become a proper periodical, one that appears predictably each year. As is usual in New Zealand, it has taken some sheilas to actually get something done: Tina Engels-Schwarzpaul of AUT's School of Art and Design has been a driving force behind the title's revival, and Julia Gatley of Auckland University's School of Architecture has her typically energetic commitment to the cause'. (*Architecture New Zealand*, April 2008, p 112)
4. In Australia, journals are ranked. In the latest research assessment, *Interstices* became one of four Australasian architectural journals with an A rating.
See http://www.arc.gov.au/era/journal_list.htm

combination of a double blind refereed section, clearly distinct from the architectural and art works, non-refereed papers, reviews, translations and interviews which compose the remainder.

The recent increase in importance and impact of the research assessment exercises (or performance-based research funding in New Zealand) tends to work against non-traditional formats and forms of engagement in favour of the purely discursive, objectified style of academia. However, we believe that it is certainly worth testing the limits of current definitions. We had to fight for the continuation of the non-refereed part at some stage, and did so because we consider it vital for the relevance of *Interstices* beyond the academic environment. We've won that battle, so far.

Since issue 02, the journal has always been devoted to a theme, which is announced in a call for papers. It provides authors with a challenge to respond to. We usually ask for suggestions of themes in advance from the editorial board and other associates, which are then discussed by a local team. The theme might be derived from current theoretical debates – either recently published books or works, or visiting academics or practitioners – from issues arising out of practice, or from themes relevant to teaching. 'Stones' and 'Particulars', the themes of the second and third issues, arose from my own research interests, which turned out to be of interest to other colleagues in their writing or teaching. *Interstices 04*, 'Accessories', was developed as a conference theme by a local group to coincide with a visit to the antipodes by Beatriz Colomina, Mark Wigley, Jennifer Bloomer and Robert Segrest. The conference papers were published in CD-Rom format. 'Faciality', issue 05, was suggested by a colleague in the Italian Department, Laurence Simmons, in response to the same theme in Deleuze and Guattari's *Thousand Plateaus* (Year Zero: Faciality, White Wall, Black Hole). 'Animal/Impulse', the theme for the first issue under joint editorship between the University of Auckland and AUT University, was a cross-breeding of suggestions to engage with Giorgio Agamben and Pierre Klossowski's interpretation of 'the combat of the impulses' in Nietzsche, crafted in the discussions of the local *Interstices* team.[5] 'Genius/Genealogy' (issue 07) reflected an ongoing interest in Agamben's work, combined with notions of genealogy (Foucault) and whakapapa (Maori and Pasifika thought). 'Disagreement' (issue 08) was again a timely suggestion by Laurence Simmons, which saw us engaging with Jacques Rancière's thinking well before anyone else in Australasia at that level. 'Expats' (issue 09), engaged with aspects of migration, alienation and exile, was the suggestion of an ex-University of Auckland student, now an assistant professor at Penn. The production of this issue confronted us with a significant divergence in the forms of practice, if not value systems, between North America and New Zealand. Indeed, our systems proved so incompatible that the initially planned joint issue editorship between the University of Auckland and Penn could eventually not be realised. The following issue, 'Adam's House in the Pacific' (issue 10), arose from a symposium in honour of Joseph Rykwert's visit to Australasia and revisits issues raised by his *Adam's House in Paradise*. 'The Traction of Drawing' (issue 11) was again shaped by the *Interstices* team on the ground. Devoted to drawing, it derived from a symposium led by Marco Frascari as keynote speaker. With this issue we initiated a category of refereed drawings. The conception of and call for papers for 'Unsettled Containers: Aspects of Interiority' (issue 12) is by Tina Engels-Schwarzpaul. The symposium featured David Leatherbarrow as keynote. Ultimately, while we always bear a

5. The regular team since issue 06 includes Jessica Barter, Carl Douglas, Tina Engels-Schwarzpaul, Julia Gatley, Mark Jackson, Albert Refiti, Laurence Simmons and myself.

professional, academic and public audience in mind, it would be fair to say that we succumb to what seems the most attractive theme likely to invite lively and topical contributions.

We plan to continue the thematic format because we have found it creates a synergy between different sectors of architecture and related arts. Without a theme, their particular concerns and contributions could end up merely juxtaposed, with no cross-fertilisation taking place. Since we rotate issue editorship on a regular basis, themed issues also have a great advantage in allowing us to focus discussion around the strengths and expertise of the respective issue editors.

Interstices, unlike many other academic journals, falls into refereed and non-refereed parts. One of the editorial board members, Anthony Hoete, was an early advocate of this format and suggested that, if it were to become a success, the journal had to offer meaty articles alongside papers that 'one can read at the back of a bus'. Only in the refereed part do we insist on the contributions' engagement with the theme, to give the theoretical discourse some cohesion and allow cross-references to emerge. This makes for sustained reading, closer to what one would expect of a book publication, which ideally gives each issue a longer-term value. Contributions to the non-refereed part can be thematically more independent, thus allowing responses, polemics and opinions on topical issues to occur without restriction. However, this part also often contains shorter, more journalistic, artistic and performative engagements with the overall theme of an issue. Reviews of books and projects, as well as

6. Translations have included, for example, Hubert Damisch, 'The Other "ich" or the Desire for the Void: For a Tomb of Adolf Loos'; Felix Guattari, 'Architectural Enunciation'; Giorgio Agamben, 'Genius'; Daniel Payot, 'The Judgement of Architecture'.

carefully selected translations further enrich this part,[6] which is also the place where we cultivate our connection with those in the profession who have an interest in theory and writing. Even though most papers and articles have so far arisen out of calls for papers, which we publish widely through various lists and websites, we also accept unsolicited contributions.

In reviving *Interstices* in 2004, we took a decision to make high production values a central part of the publication format. To make the best use of our limited budget, we decided to publish in black and white only, but on high-quality stock with excellent printers.[7] This is important because we envisage the publication going well beyond text: images are crucial and we experiment regularly with alternative production processes. However, until now, we have not made optimal use of the potential resulting from that editorial decision.

The preceding seminar, lecture series or, more recently, symposium, gives postgraduate students and emergent researchers a chance to develop their work in stages and receive comment before further development for publication. Any possible polarity between teacher and editor, or creator and curator, therefore appears to us to be artificial: all editors are also writers, artists, teachers, architectural practitioners or even curators – one has to be creative to succeed in any of these engagements. Thus, planning for a forthcoming issue of *Interstices* can reflect concerns with curriculum development along shared areas of interest (study for the students, research for the teachers, and the provision of an area of engagement where these can happen). This was the case, for instance, for 'Animal/Impulse', where 'Impulse' was the theme of a lecture

7. This follows an established, if somewhat neglected, Kiwi intellectual tradition: New Zealand born-Lord Rutherford famously inspired his team on one occasion with the remark 'We haven't the money, so we've got to think!' (1962 Brunel Lecture, 14 February 1962).

series and resulting studio experiments. Incidentally, a theme also enables colleagues to share resources around research topics and provides them with an intellectual peer group, which makes academic explorations so much more productive. Without such collaborations, *Interstices* could not appear on a regular annual basis. Obviously, such lively and multi-faceted endeavours need the midwifery of a permanent editorial team to make sure the birth actually happens.

In this sparsely populated part of the world, remote from the centres of architectural debate, a critical mass is needed to achieve sufficient momentum. This we achieve through an openness to changing and different collaborations in several respects (openness to concerns and needs beyond our institutions, beyond our disciplines, and beyond New Zealand and Australia, into the Pacific and further). A position on the periphery of the architectural world can sometimes provide us with a special type of perception. What is missing or excluded from the centre often re-emerges at the periphery but there is also something native to the periphery that the centre does not see. It is one's peripheral vision which first detects movement. Ours is not a 20/20 vision. Close to ideas and practices of building and space quite different from those of the 'western world', our reading of architecture may also produce different propositions. In this doubly peripheral field of vision, some phenomena sometimes appear clearer than in the central cone of vision.

BIOGRAPHIES

An Architektur was founded in 2002 continuing the work of the architecture collective Freies Fach – a group that since the mid-1990s had sought to critically assess the restrictive reconstruction of Berlin through actions, exhibitions and publications. *An Architektur* is the exercise of discursive architectural practice. For us, both the critical analysis of spatial relations and the visualisation of their inherent conceptions offer a possibility of political agency. In thematic issues, socio-political criteria are applied to concrete examples and questions of architecture. *An Architektur* exposes the social and political implications of topics that tend to be discussed too introspectively within the domain of architecture and its relevance to everyday life. In 2004 *An Architektur* organised the first 'Camp for Oppositional Architecture' in Berlin, which was carried forward in 2006 in Utrecht and in 2009 as 'Ten Days for Oppositional Architecture' in New York. Currently active editorial board members are Oliver Clemens, Jesko Fezer, Sabine Horlitz, Anita Kaspar and Andreas Müller.

Haig Beck and Jackie Cooper arrived in London in 1969. Haig was accepted into the AA Diploma School at the same time as landing a job with the *Architects' Journal*. He did both. They married in 1970. Jackie studied Communications, graduated in 1972, and joined the AA's new Communications Studio, headed by Dennis Crompton. Haig was appointed co-editor of *Architectural Design* in 1976, and sole editor in 1977. He left *AD* in 1979, and Jackie left the AA, to found *International Architect* magazine, which they independently edited and published until returning to Australia in 1986. Haig is a professor at the University of Melbourne. In 1996 they launched *UME*, a magazine about architectural drawings, publishing 21 editions. *UME* 22, in

production, is a 260-page *oeuvre complète* of Andresen
O'Gorman. *UME* is now available free online:
www.umemagazine.com. Writings include monographs on
Glenn Murcutt; Denton Corker Marshall; Tract landscape
architects; Architectus; contribution to Phaidon's *10x10:
10 Critics 100 Architects*, 2000. Now writing a book on the
world's first tensegrity bridge, Kurilpa Bridge in Brisbane.

Marcus Carter received his Bachelor of Architecture
from the University of Kansas and his Master of Architecture
from Yale University. While at Yale, he was a teaching
fellow in urban history and was co-editor of the *Yale
Architecture Journal, Perspecta 38: Architecture After All*.
Marcus has worked in internationally renowned design firms
in New York City including Robert AM Stern Architects,
Kohn Pederson Fox, and Steven Holl Architects. He has
engaged in projects around the world of diverse size and type
including private residences, institutional projects, mixed-use
towers, and urban design proposals. Marcus also collaborates
on design research with Christopher Lee as CLAD. He is a
LEED Accredited Professional and a registered architect in
New York. He is also a member of the Architectural League
of New York and the Society of Architectural Historians.
Marcus lives with his wife in Brooklyn.

Cynthia Davidson is the founder and editor of *Log,
Observations on Architecture and the Contemporary City*,
a tri-annual journal published by the Anyone Corporation
in New York City. Also the founding director of the Anyone
project, she was editor of the architecture tabloid *ANY* (or
Architecture New York) from 1993 to 2000, and editor
of the ten Any books (*Anyone, Anyplace, Anything*, etc),
which documented the ten international Any architecture
conferences on the undecidability of architecture at the
end of the millennium (1991 to 2000). Prior to the Anyone

project she edited *Inland Architect*, a regional magazine based in Chicago. In addition to editing *Log*, Ms Davidson is also editor of the *Writing Architecture Series* books, which emphasise architectural theory, published with MIT Press. A former Loeb Fellow in Advanced Environmental Studies at Harvard's Graduate School of Design, she studied journalism and art history as an undergraduate at Ohio Wesleyan.

Salomon Frausto directs the public programmes of the Berlage Institute in Rotterdam, where he is also the editor of its flagship publication *Hunch*. He graduated with degrees in architecture from the University of Michigan and Columbia University. From 2001–07 he coordinated the public and scholarly programmes of the Temple Hoyne Buell Center for the Study of American Architecture at Columbia University. He is co-editor, with Joan Ockman, of *Architourism: Authentic, Exotic, Escapist, Spectacular* (Prestel, 2005). He is presently completing an anthology titled *The Berlage Global Survey of the Culture, Education and Practice of Architecture and Urbanism*. In early 2011 he will launch *XYZ*, an experimental mobile tablet publication for the advancement of architecture discourse through the use of new media technology. The publication will feature specifically commissioned material by architects, critics and scholars as well as curate existing web-based content related to the built environment.

Izabel Gass received her BA and BArch from Rice University. After working at Venturi, Scott Brown & Associates, she returned to the Rice School of Architecture to oversee the school's publications and teach architectural theory seminars, including courses such as, Design and Knowledge Production, as well as a historical survey of the journal *Assemblage*. She is now a PhD student in the History of Art department at Yale University.

Christoph Grafe is an architect and writer based in Amsterdam, London and Bremen, and Associate Professor of Architectural Design/Interior at TU Delft. A graduate of TU Delft, he subsequently worked in practice in Amsterdam and studied in the Histories and Theories programme at the Architectural Association School in London. His PhD dissertation focused on the architecture of postwar public buildings for culture. The book *Cafés and Bars – The architecture of sociability* (co-edited with Franziska Bollerey) was published in 2007. Grafe is a member of the editorial board of the *Journal of Architecture* and the editorial advisory board of *Interiors* (Berg publishers). He has been an editor of *OASE* since 1992.

Jeffrey Inaba is the founder of INABA, an architecture firm based in Los Angeles. Its recent projects include urban design, housing and installation projects in Europe, Asia and the US for clients that include the Whitney Museum of American Art, Storefront for Art and Architecture, New Museum, Pacific Foundation, Public Art Fund and the City of Miami. He also directs the Columbia Laboratory for Architectural Broadcasting (C-Lab), a research and policy unit at Columbia University's Graduate School of Architecture, Planning and Preservation that investigates urban and architecture issues that are of public consequence. He is the Features Editor of *Volume* magazine and the author of numerous publications, including the recent book, *World of Giving* (Lars Müller Publishers, 2010). Inaba received a Master of Architecture with Distinction and MA in Philosophy of Architecture degrees from Harvard University, and a BA with Highest Honours from University of California, Berkeley.

Ross Jenner is Deputy Head (Research) of the School of Architecture, University of Auckland. He has practised in Britain, Finland, Switzerland and New Zealand, where he continues to practise. He has a PhD from the University of Pennsylvania on Italian Rationalism. He has taught at several universities in Australia and the United States. With students and other members of faculty, he designed and built the Auckland School's winning entry to the 1991 Biennale di Venezia, recipient of the Venice Prize. He was Commissioner for the New Zealand Section of the XIX Triennale di Milano. His writing and design have been published in numerous books and journals, including *Transition, Architecture Australia, Lotus, The Journal of Architecture*. He is currently working on a book on Italian architecture between Futurism and Rationalism. With Tina Engels-Schwarzpaul, he is executive editor of *Interstices, Journal of Architecture and Related Arts*, which he initiated.

Tahl Kaminer is an assistant professor at the Delft School of Design (TU Delft). He has completed a doctoral research tying architecture to the social via the 1970s disciplinary crisis, and received a MSc in Architecture History and Theory at the Bartlett, UCL in 2003. Tahl is a founding member of 66 East, Centre for Urban Culture, an Amsterdam-based foundation involved in the study of the urban environment, and co-founded *Footprint*, the DSD academic journal. In 2011 Routledge will publish Tahl's book *Architecture, Crisis, and Resuscitation: The Reproduction of Post-Fordism in Late-Twentieth-Century Architecture*. He has recently co-edited and contributed to the volumes *Critical Tools* (La Lettre Volée, 2011) and *Houses in Transformation: Interventions in European Gentrification* (NAi Publishers, 2008), and is currently co-editing the forthcoming volume *Urban Asymmetries* (010 Publishers, 2011).

Silvia Kolbowski is an artist whose scope of address includes the ethics of history, culture and the unconscious. Her project After Hiroshima Mon Amour (2004–08) was installed at LA><Art, LA, Ellen Gallery, Montreal, Museum of Modern Art, Ljubjlana, and screened internationally. Her 1998/99 project An Inadequate History of Conceptual Art was part of the 1999 Whitney Biennial, and installed in many other venues, including the Oliver Art Center, Oakland, the Centre for Contemporary Art, Warsaw, and the Villa Arson, Nice. A recent project, Dear Silvia, has been produced in both audio and print format by *Fillip* journal, Vancouver. In addition, Kolbowski has worked in an editorial capacity with art and architecture journals, including as co-editor of *October* journal from 1993–2000 (currently still on their Advisory Board), and as editor of *Scapes* journal from 2000–05. A new project will be exhibited in the 2010 Taipei Biennial.

Michael Kubo is pursuing a PhD in History, Theory and Criticism of Architecture at MIT. He is a curator at pinkcomma gallery in Boston, where he recently exhibited Publishing Practices (2009), a study of publishing and editorial practices by architects in the past century; with Chris Grimley and Mark Pasnik, he is co-curator of HEROIC: Boston Concrete 1957–1976 (2009) and the inaugural Design Biennial Boston (2010). He worked with Actar in Barcelona from 2002 to 2006 and in New York as director of Actar Publishers from 2006 to 2008. With Farshid Moussavi, he is the author of *The Function of Ornament*; other editorial projects include Kazys Varnelis's *The Infrastructural City: Networked Ecologies in Los Angeles*, Sanford Kwinter's *Far From Equilibrium*, and the *Verb* boogazine series. He has taught at Pratt Institute, the University of Texas at Austin, and SUNY Buffalo, where he was the Reyner Banham Fellow for 2008–09.

Johan Lagae graduated as an engineer-architect at the Department of Architecture and Urban Planning, Ghent University (1991) where he is currently teaching Architectural History of the Twentieth Century with a particular focus on the non-European context. He holds a PhD on twentieth-century colonial architecture in the former Belgian Congo (2002). His current research focuses on transnational networks of building and planning expertise in postwar Africa, on Central African urban history and on the issue of built heritage in postcolonial Africa. He has published widely in international journals (*Journal of Architecture, Third Text*) and edited volumes, and contributed to a number of exhibitions on the Congo. His most recent publications are *Congo belge en images* (with Carl De Keyzer, 2010), *Kinshasa. Architecture et paysage urbains* (with Bernard Toulier and Marc Gemoets, 2010) and *l'Afrique c'est chic: Architecture and Planning in Africa 1950–1970* (*OASE* #82, with Tom Avermaete). He has been a member of the editorial board of *OASE* since 2003.

Christopher Marcinkoski is Assistant Professor at the University of Pennsylvania School of Design and director of PORT Architecture + Urbanism, a leading-edge research and design practice based in New York and Chicago. PORT's work has received significant recognition, including commendations by the Van Alen Institute and Dessau's Bauhaus Foundation. In 2009 PORT won the WPA 2.0 infrastructure design competition organised by UCLA/cityLAB. Prior to his appointment at PENN, he was a senior associate at James Corner Field Operations, where he led the office's large-scale planning and urban design work, including the Qian Hai Water City, Shelby Farms Park, the San Juan Knowledge Corridor and the West Side Rail Yards masterplan. He holds a BArch from the Pennsylvania State University and an MArch from Yale University, receiving both schools' highest awards for design. He was co-editor of the *Yale Architecture Journal, Perspecta 38: Architecture After All.*

Reinhold Martin is Associate Professor of Architecture in the Graduate School of Architecture, Planning, and Preservation at Columbia University, where he directs the PhD programme in architecture, and the Temple Hoyne Buell Center for the Study of American Architecture. He is a founding co-editor of the journal *Grey Room* and has published widely on the history and theory of modern and contemporary architecture. He is the author of *The Organizational Complex: Architecture, Media, and Corporate Space* (MIT Press, 2003), and the co-author, with Kadambari Baxi, of *Multi-National City: Architectural Itineraries* (Actar, 2007). His new book on postmodernism, *Utopia's Ghost*, was published by the University of Minnesota Press in 2010.

Joanna Merwood-Salisbury is Assistant Professor of Architecture at the School of Constructed Environments, Parsons The New School for Design in New York City. An architect by training, she received her PhD in architectural history and theory from Princeton University in 2003. The author of *Chicago 1890: The Skyscraper and the Modern City* (University of Chicago Press, 2009), she has published widely on architecture and design in a number of journals including *Journal of the Society of Architectural Historians, Journal of Architectural Education, Technology and Culture, Design Issues, Grey Room* and *Lotus International*. The editor of *Scapes* from 2006–09, she presently sits on the editorial board of *AA Files*.

Amanda Reeser Lawrence is a founding co-editor, along with Ashley Schafer, of the architectural journal *PRAXIS*. A licensed architect, critic and historian, she is Assistant Professor of Design at the School of Architecture at Northeastern. She received her PhD in architectural history and theory from Harvard University's Graduate School of Design, a Master of Architecture from Columbia University and her BA Summa Cum Laude from Princeton University. Her current research focuses on the British architect James Stirling (1924–92), and her book *James Stirling: Revisionary Modernist* will be published by Yale University Press in the autumn of 2012. Her research has been funded by the Paul Mellon Center for Studies in British Art and the Graduate Society at Harvard University.

William S Saunders is the founding editor of the *Harvard Design Magazine* at the Harvard University Graduate School of Design. He is the author of *Modern Architecture: Photographs by Ezra Stoller* and editor of several books including *Urban Design* (with Alex Krieger); *Nature, Landscape, and Building for Sustainability*; *The New Architectural Pragmatism*; *Judging Architectural Value*; *Urban Planning Today*; *Sprawl and Suburbia*; and *Commodification and Spectacle in Architecture*, as well as articles on Rem Koolhaas's writing, judgement of architecture, Christopher Alexander's writing, and poetry of the 1960s and 1970s.

Jonathan D Solomon is an American architect based in Hong Kong, where he is Assistant Professor and Acting Head of the Department of Architecture at the University of Hong Kong. Solomon, with Emily Abruzzo, is a founding editor of 306090 Books, a publication series featuring novel developments in architecture, landscape architecture and urbanism that published its 13th volume, *Sustain and Develop*, in 2009. He has written for publications including *Log* (New York), *Footprint* (Delft), and *Urban China* (Beijing); and is the author of *Pamphlet Architecture #26, 13 Projects for the Sheridan Expressway* (Princeton Architectural Press,

2004). Solomon has taught design at the City College of New York and, as a Banham Fellow, at the University at Buffalo.

Lukasz Stanek graduated in architecture and philosophy in Kraków, Weimar and Münster. After defending his dissertation at the Delft University of Technology, and fellowships at the Jan van Eyck Academie (Maastricht) and the Institut d'Urbanisme de Paris, he is currently a researcher at the Chair of Architecture Theory, Swiss Federal Institute of Technology (ETH) in Zurich. He organised two conferences about the theory of Henri Lefebvre and urban research today, www.henrilefebvre.org. His book *Henri Lefebvre on Space: Architecture, Urban Research and the Production of Theory* will be published in 2011 (University of Minnesota Press). He was the curator of the exhibition PRL™ Export Architecture and Urbanism from Socialist Poland (Warsaw Museum of Modern Art, 2010). He is responsible for the research programme about the transfer of knowledge in architecture, planning and building technology from the socialist East and the capitalist West towards the post-colonial South during the Cold War, www.south-of-eastwest.net.

Neyran Turan is an Assistant Professor at Rice University School of Architecture. She has recently received her doctoral degree from Harvard University Graduate School of Design (GSD). Turan holds a masters degree from Yale University School of Architecture and a Bachelor of Architecture degree from Istanbul Technical University. Turan's work focuses on contemporary interpretations of scale, infrastructure and form, and their potentiality for new positionings in architecture and urbanism. She is the cofounder of NEMEstudio, a research and design collaborative based in Houston and Boston, and the founding chief-editor of the recently launched Harvard GSD journal *New Geographies*.

Thomas Weaver works at the Architectural Association School of Architecture in London as editor of *AA Files* and as a tutor on the school's History and Critical Thinking MA. He has previously edited *ANY* magazine in New York and writes regularly on architecture for various books and journals. In addition to the AA School he has taught architectural design and history at Princeton University and the Cooper Union.

Mason White is an architect, writer and educator based in Toronto, Canada. He is Assistant Professor at the University of Toronto Daniels Faculty of Architecture, Landscape, and Design. White received a BArch from Virginia Tech and MArch II from Harvard Graduate School of Design. He is a founding partner of Lateral Office in 2003 with Lola Sheppard, and a director of InfraNet Lab, launched in 2008. Lateral Office has won or been shortlisted for competitions internationally, most recently the WPA 2.0 competition (2009) and Pamphlet Architecture #30 (2009), and has a publication forthcoming from Princeton Architectural Press (2010). At InfraNet Lab, he is a curator of HYDROCity: Hydrology and Urbanism (2009/10) and a founder of the recently launched *[bracket]* (Actar, 2010).

Kirk Wooller is an architect and researcher based in Chicago, where he is director of the research and design practice, Remake Architecture. He holds a BArch and MArch from the University of Auckland and an MA (Histories & Theories) and PhD from the Architectural Association. His doctoral thesis explores the diminishing role of judgement in contemporary architectural publications and the implications this has for the innovation of architectural knowledge. He has practised in Auckland, New York and London and taught at the Architectural Association, University of Brighton and University of Auckland. He has organised several exhibitions and symposia, including the AA PhD Dialogues annual international doctoral research symposium (2008–09). He has also been the recipient of the Frederick Ost Scholarship, the William Chick Masters Scholarship and the William Chick Doctoral Scholarship in Architecture.

Arthur Wortmann studied architecture at the Eindhoven University of Technology, and History and Theory of Architecture at the Architectural Association Graduate School in London. He is currently managing editor of *Mark*, an Amsterdam-based international architecture magazine he helped to found in 2005. Before that, he was editor of *Archis* and lecturer at several architecture schools. He published numerous articles and contributed to many books. From 2000 to 2005 he was editor of the *Architecture in the Netherlands* yearbook.

COLOPHON

20/20: Editorial Takes on Architectural Discourse

Edited by Kirk Wooller
Art Director: Zak Kyes
Design: Wayne Daly
Editorial Assistant: Clare Barrett

Printed in Denmark by Norhaven A/S

ISBN 978-1-907896-00-2 ᴇxᴄᴀᴛ

For a catalogue of AA Publications visit
www.aaschool.ac.uk/publications
or email publications@aaschool.ac.uk

AA Publications, 36 Bedford Square
London WC1B 3ES
T + 44 (0)20 7887 4021
F + 44 (0)20 7414 0783

720·5 TWE